The Next Supreme Leader

Succession in the Islamic Republic of Iran

Alireza Nader, David E. Thaler, S. R. Bohandy

Prepared for the Office of the Secretary of Defense

Approved for public release; distribution unlimited

NATIONAL DEFENSE RESEARCH INSTITUTE

The research described in this report was prepared for the Office of the Secretary of Defense (OSD). The research was conducted within the RAND National Defense Research Institute, a federally funded research and development center sponsored by OSD, the Joint Staff, the Unified Combatant Commands, the Navy, the Marine Corps, the defense agencies, and the defense Intelligence Community under Contract W74V8H-06-C-0002.

Library of Congress Cataloging-in-Publication Data

Nader, Alireza.
  The next supreme leader : succession in the Islamic Republic of Iran / Alireza Nader, David E. Thaler, S. R. Bohandy.
    p. cm.
  Includes bibliographical references.
  ISBN 978-0-8330-5133-2 (pbk. : alk. paper)
    1. Heads of state—Succession—Iran. 2. Iran—Politics and government—1997- I. Thaler, David E. II. Bohandy, S. R. III. Title.

JQ1786.N33 2011
  320.955—dc22

                                                                    2011002805

The RAND Corporation is a nonprofit institution that helps improve policy and decisionmaking through research and analysis. RAND's publications do not necessarily reflect the opinions of its research clients and sponsors.

RAND® is a registered trademark.

Cover photo: Iran's Supreme Leader Ayatollah Ali Khamenei in Tehran to deliver a speech, with a picture of the late spiritual leader, Ayatollah Khomeini, on the wall behind (AP).

Published 2011 by the RAND Corporation
1776 Main Street, P.O. Box 2138, Santa Monica, CA 90407-2138
1200 South Hayes Street, Arlington, VA 22202-5050
4570 Fifth Avenue, Suite 600, Pittsburgh, PA 15213-2665
RAND URL: http://www.rand.org/
To order RAND documents or to obtain additional information, contact
Distribution Services: Telephone: (310) 451-7002;
Fax: (310) 451-6915; Email: order@rand.org

Preface

As the commander in chief and highest political authority in Iran, the current Supreme Leader, Ayatollah Ali Khamenei, has played a critical role in the direction of the Islamic Republic of Iran. This has never been more true than during the tumultuous 2009 presidential elections, the outcome of which was determined by Khamenei's decisive support of President Mahmoud Ahmadinejad.

Only two men have held the position of Supreme Leader since the Islamic Republic of Iran was established in 1979: Khamenei and his predecessor, Ayatollah Ruhollah Khomeini. These two leaders are characterized by widely disparate personalities, leadership skills, and political instincts. Khomeini was scholarly, iconic, and charismatic, creating and sustaining the position of Supreme Leader through his personal standing. In contrast, Khamenei has relied on alliance-building, patronage, and the vast bureaucracy controlled by the Supreme Leader's office to maintain and expand his influence. As Khamenei ages, and as rumors of his ill health intensify, U.S. policymakers and analysts need to consider the various scenarios for what may follow after he passes from the scene. The eventual outcome—what the office of the Supreme Leader looks like in Khamenei's wake—will determine the Islamic Republic's direction.

The research documented in this report identifies three key factors that will shape succession of the next Supreme Leader and outlines alternative scenarios for the post-Khamenei era. For each of the factors, it provides a set of indicators that observers can use to assess the most important trends. It situates all of this within the context of the June

2009 election. The study, which assumes a working understanding of the Islamic Republic's system of government and some of its history, should be of interest to analysts, as well as policymakers and other observers of Iran.[1]

This research was sponsored by the Office of the Secretary of Defense and conducted within the Intelligence Policy Center of the RAND National Defense Research Institute, a federally funded research and development center sponsored by the Office of the Secretary of Defense, the Joint Staff, the Unified Combatant Commands, the Navy, the Marine Corps, the defense agencies, and the defense Intelligence Community.

For more information on the RAND Intelligence Policy Center, see http://www.rand.org/nsrd/about/intel.html or contact the director (contact information is provided on the web page).

---

[1]   For background on Iran's political system, see David E. Thaler, Alireza Nader, Shahram Chubin, Jerrold D. Green, Charlotte Lynch, and Frederic Wehrey, *Mullahs, Guards, and Bonyads: An Exploration of Iranian Leadership Dynamics*, Santa Monica, Calif.: RAND Corporation, MG-878-OSD, 2010.

Contents

Figures

Summary

The 2009 presidential election in the Islamic Republic of Iran was one of the most transformative events in Iran's modern history. It bared important schisms within the *nezam* (political system) and pitted two key camps against one another, each with a very different vision of what Iran should be and what it should become. It appeared to solidify (at least for the near future) the dominance of the hard-line faction of the Islamist Right under President Mahmoud Ahmadinejad and continued an ongoing militarization of Iranian politics led by the Islamic Revolutionary Guards Corps, firmly entrenching a more insular cadre of decisionmakers at the *nezam*'s core. The widespread fraud alleged by the leading opposition candidate, former Prime Minister Mir Hossein Mousavi, and the *nezam*'s repressive response irrevocably shattered an unspoken contract between the government and the people—one in which the theocratic government had allowed some popular political participation and limited personal space in return for the people's acquiescence to the status quo.

Even the highest authority in Iran, the Supreme Leader, Ayatollah Ali Khamenei, did not escape censure by the opposition—a traditional "red line" in Iranian politics that clerics, politicians, and voters alike crossed numerous times after the polls closed. Previously, Khamenei had portrayed himself as above the often-brutal factional "fray" in Iran. But now he came down decisively on the side of Ahmadinejad and his hard-line allies and used the Revolutionary Guards to preserve the status quo. In so doing, he altered the role of the office he occupied, which had been created by the father of the revolution, Ayatollah Ruhollah Khomeini.

The Supreme Leader is the linchpin of the Islamic Republic: He guides its character, policies, and approach to the outside world. Khamenei is 71 and rumored to be in ill health.[1] Were he to pass away and a succession battle to ensue, the outcome could change the nature of Iran for better or for worse from the U.S. perspective. Because it is patently difficult to predict such an outcome, U.S. analysts and policymakers must prepare for alternative possibilities for succession. To address this challenge, this report has a twofold objective: First, it sheds light on how the position and role of the Supreme Leader might change after Khamenei leaves the scene. Second, it points to indicators that can provide insight into what seems to be the most likely direction for the future succession at any given time. Because the context in which succession would occur becomes more uncertain the further into the future one looks, we focus on the near term—i.e., a succession that would take place within the next two to three years. However, we also speculate about the changes that are likely to ensue in the longer term if Khamenei remains Supreme Leader for the next ten years or more.

To arrive at our conclusions, we conducted a historical analysis of both the institution of Supreme Leader and key aspects of Khomeini's and Khamenei's terms in the position. After examining the justifications for the creation of the Supreme Leader position during the Islamic Revolution, we analyzed the position's constitutional and informal powers and how Khomeini and Khamenei have used these powers. We also explored various debates and political and religious discourses in Iran about the nature of the Supreme Leader, including those surrounding the 1989 succession.

On the basis of this research, we identified a set of three primary factors that will shape the next succession and determine what happens to the institution of the Supreme Leader. In conjunction, we pinpointed indicators that can be used to track how each factor is evolving. Finally, we developed five scenarios that seem to have the greatest relevance, given the historical Iranian discourse on this subject, and

---

[1]   As of January 2011.

analyzed the influence the key factors might have on the relative likelihood that any of these scenarios would occur.

Three Key Factors Will Shape the Next Succession

Three factors will have a decisive influence on the nature of the next Supreme Leader—or even whether there will be a Supreme Leader to follow Khamenei—at the time of the next succession:

- the factions and personalities in positions of power and influence
- the prevailing concept of *velayat-e faghih* (rule of the supreme jurisprudent), which forms the ideological and political basis of the Islamic Republic as it exists today
- the decisions and actions of Khamenei's "personal network."

How the three factors are configured at the time of succession will have a huge impact on the nature of the next Supreme Leader. By *configuration*, we mean the driving features and prominence of each of the factors in relation to the others. The configuration is fluid; it has evolved several times, even during Khamenei's rule.

Iran is in a state of great societal, religious, and political transformation. The Green Movement (formed in response to the 2009 presidential election), the women's rights movement, Iran's declining economy, and Iranian relations with the United States could all also play a role in determining the outcome of the next succession. However, our focus is succession in the near term, as it would take place in the current political system. The three factors we have identified as the most important in shaping it are all defining elements of the Islamic Republic's *nezam* as it exists today. Should the succession take place in the longer term—within a decade or two—a number of those other factors may indeed come to assume a more decisive role.

Factor 1: The Factional Balance of Power

The Islamic Republic's competing factions have a deep and vested interest in shaping the next succession. Iranian history has been characterized by backroom politics, especially since the Islamic Republic was established in 1979. Despite the formal rules established by the Iranian constitution, the *nezam*'s factionalism and informal style of decision-making continue to reflect a weakness of official political institutions throughout Iranian history. The next Supreme Leader's succession will be determined within this informal and often nontransparent system.

Factions in Iran today can be broadly divided into the Islamist Right and the Islamist Left. Power struggles not only between these groups but also, especially, within them are a hallmark of contemporary politics in the Islamic Republic. Among the most important are competitions within the Islamist Right between pragmatic conservatives and principlists and between principlist subfactions.

Factional interests influenced the selection of Khamenei for Supreme Leader over the heir Khomeini had originally chosen, Ayatollah Hossein Ali Montazeri, during the 1989 succession. Khamenei met Khomeini's and the Islamist Right's ideological and administrative qualifications for Supreme Leader and in many ways was Montazeri's opposite. But factionalism will play an even bigger role in the next succession than in 1989. Khomeini's supreme authority and iconic status allowed him to designate his successor without much opposition from the Islamic Republic's competing factions. But Khomeini's death and Khamenei's tenure in office led to increased factionalism and early signs of political fragmentation within the *nezam*. This has been especially true under the presidencies of Mohammad Khatami and Mahmoud Ahmadinejad. Unlike Khomeini, Khamenei has clearly taken sides with the hard-line principlists within the Islamist Right. If Khamenei were to die soon, the principlists would be well positioned to shape the next succession, especially after Ahmadinejad's reelection in June 2009.

Factor 2: *Velayat-e Faghih*

Iran's *nezam* derives its religious and political legitimacy from the concept of *velayat-e faghih*, which underpins the Supreme Leader's authority. *Velayat-e faghih* has historically been an apolitical concept in Shi'a Islam, providing the clergy with religious stewardship of the people—and some temporal authority over the weak, orphaned, and infirm—

in the absence of the 12th Imam, who is believed to have gone into hiding or occultation. This apolitical view of *velayat-e faghih* is frequently referred to as the "traditionalist" or "quietist" school of thought on the subject.

Khomeini reinterpreted *velayat-e faghih* to form the basis of an Islamic state led by the clergy. Two broad schools of thought have since developed under Khomeini's reinterpretation: the "absolutist" and the "democratic." Islamist Right proponents of the former view the Supreme Leader's authority as absolute and derived from divine will, a reading closely associated with Khomeini's. In contrast, those who favor the democratic view of the concept believe that the Supreme Leader must be popular as well as pious and derive his authority from the people. This school of thought is associated with the Islamist Left. The traditional or quietist view of *velayat-e faghih* remains strong outside Iran, as practiced by Shi'a clergy in Najaf, but also in Qom.

The concept of *velayat-e faghih* prevalent among the clergy during the succession period will shape their views regarding the next Supreme Leader. With Khamenei's passing, the competition between the absolutist, democratic, and quietist views on *velayat-e faghih* is likely to intensify. Khamenei's authoritarian rule, his reliance on *velayat-e faghih* to ensure his personal authority, and *velayat-e faghih*'s association with the hard-line Islamist Right have weakened its legitimacy among the key elements of the clergy and political elite, as well as broad segments of the Iranian population.

Factor 3: Khamenei's Personal Network
Lacking the religious and political legitimacy of his predecessor, Khamenei has maintained his power and influence through a personal network that bypasses and overshadows formally elected decisionmaking bodies. This network includes the sizable Office of the Supreme Leader; a web of special representatives throughout the government, military, and society; and key clerical and military institutions, such as the Revolutionary Guards. This personal network acts as Khamenei's "eyes and ears" throughout the *nezam* and enables him to shape Iran's domestic and foreign policies, despite the opposition of various factions and power centers. The network, and the Supreme Leader himself,

have become openly wedded to relatively narrow factional interests. Its members will want to protect those interests in the next succession.

The 2009 election vividly demonstrated this factor at work, when Khamenei endorsed Ahmadinejad as president under highly controversial circumstances, and his personal network acted decisively to preserve the status quo against what it described as a "velvet revolution" led by the opposition and supported by outside powers. Just days before the voting, General Yadollah Javani, the Revolutionary Guards' political bureau chief, announced that the Guards would act to "snuff out" any attempts at a velvet revolution. In the election's immediate aftermath, the Guards and the Basij militia were used to put down large-scale opposition protests after taking over internal security.

Today, hard-liners within the Revolutionary Guards have arguably become the most powerful component of Khamenei's personal network. They and other members of the network may act decisively to prevent an "unfavorable" Supreme Leader from being selected, even if he is elected through constitutional means by the Assembly of Experts. In addition, with his endorsement of Ahmadinejad, Khamenei broke with the Supreme Leader's traditional role of standing "above the fray" of factional politics. As a result, he can no longer claim a broad-based constituency, and this too will have consequences in a future succession.

Five Succession Scenarios Best Cover the Range of Possibilities

Given our analysis of the key factors and leadership concepts that have been discussed in Iran, five scenarios describing different end states for succession of the Supreme Leader, Ayatollah Ali Khamenei, over the next two to three years seem to best represent the spectrum of possibilities. All of the scenarios are plausible, although they are not equally likely to come about. The likelihood of each scenario will depend on how the three key factors are configured at the time of succession. This configuration is in flux, largely propelled by the 2009 presidential election and its aftermath.

The five scenarios are as follows:

- *status quo*, in which Khamenei is followed by a leader like himself, possibly someone he handpicks
- *absolutist*, an absolute dictator, with strong religious and political credentials, supported by a cult of personality
- *democratic,* a reformist leader who is more accountable to the republican institutions and the electorate than Khamenei currently is
- *Leadership Council*, an executive leadership group that replaces a single leader
- *abolition*, the demise of the Supreme Leader position in favor of republicanism.

The first four scenarios represent leadership options that the *nezam* could at least portray as occurring within the framework of the Islamic Revolution and *velayat-e faghih*. In other words, the next Supreme Leader could make the case that the *nezam* remains founded on the legacy of Ayatollah Ruhollah Khomeini and the "true" aims of the Islamic Republic (according to the *nezam*'s interpretation). The fifth scenario, abolition, represents the demise of the Islamic Republic as it exists today. These scenarios are by no means predictive; post-Khamenei Iran is more likely to look like some adaptation of one or two of the scenarios rather than an exact replica. Their purpose, rather, is to help analysts and policymakers make sense of indications that may be related to succession.

Developments in the three key factors, and how they reconfigure in relation to each other, can be watched by analysts to determine the relative likelihood that one or more scenarios will come about as succession approaches. They can also be used as signs of maneuvering among factions and power centers for advantage in preparation for the eventual succession. For each factor, we identify a set of indicators. In the case of factional competition, these indicators include the relative power a given faction holds within key government institutions, the balance of factional representation in the *nezam*, and the relationships of given factions with the Supreme Leader. Indicators for *velayat-e faghih* include statements by clerics about divine authority and popular will, the political and religious standing of those clerics, government responses to their statements, and the use of *velayat-e faghih* by the government itself. Indicators of how the role and influence of Khamenei's personal network are evolving include the status and nature of the Revolutionary Guards, the cohesiveness of the activities of the Supreme Leader's special representatives, and the size and authorities of the Office of the Supreme Leader.

In Light of the 2009 Election, the Status Quo Scenario Seems Most Likely in the Near Term

The postelection alignment of the three factors—with the Islamist Right solidifying its dominance of elected institutions, *velayat-e faghih* seeming to lose ground as a decisive factor, and Khamenei's personal network having taken resolute action to protect the status quo—suggests strongly that the most likely succession scenario in the next few months or years is the status quo scenario. The absolutist scenario is a close second. Although possible, it is considerably less likely that any of the other three scenarios would come to fruition in the near term. We base this assessment on indications that the election reinforced the power of Khamenei's personal network and the hard-line principlist wing of the Islamist Right while considerably weakening the Islamist Left and republican institutions.

At the same time, though, we contend that the election diminished the *legitimacy* of Khamenei and the institution of the Supreme Leader, and this could very well have consequences in the longer term. The election revealed rifts within both Iran's political leadership and its clerical establishment that could eventually challenge the Supreme Leader's personal network and the currently dominant faction. The elevated likelihood of the status quo and absolutist scenarios does not preclude challenges to Khamenei from influential power centers outside his network of support.

The Likelihood of Longer-Term Succession Scenarios Is Uncertain

While predicting the course of a potential succession in the Islamic Republic (or any other major political developments, for that matter) in the very near term is already difficult, uncertainty increases exponentially the further into the future one looks. Many variables will evolve in ways that are hard to determine from the present vantage point. If succession occurs in ten, 15, or even 20 years, both external and internal forces could be at play that significantly alter the political, economic, and societal contexts in which decisions are made within the *nezam*—and how the three key factors are configured when the time for succession eventually comes.

First, the "old guard," whose several dozen members were active in spearheading the Islamic Revolution and who have held positions of power and influence in the Islamic Republic ever since, will be gone. A new cadre of leaders, many of whom came of age during the Iran-Iraq War, will have replaced their elders. They will bring with them a different perception of the Islamic Republic and different life experiences that will influence their actions and decisions.

Second, the alignment of factions, informal networks, and power centers in the Islamic Republic will change in ways difficult to predict. This goes to the heart of the configuration of all three key factors, but particularly to that of the factional balance of power and Khamenei's personal network. The Revolutionary Guards are currently the dominant political, military, and economic institution in Iran, with the election seeming to have cemented their position. But while it is difficult to see their power waning in the near future, it is not a foregone conclusion that they will dominate Iran in ten years.

Third, economic, societal, cultural, and other endogenous issues will evolve and put pressure on the *nezam* to adapt. Among the most prominent of these are providing job opportunities for a youthful population, considering the demands of Iran's women's rights movement, and dealing with the burgeoning information revolution. These and other challenges will provoke the *nezam* either to meet the expanding needs of the population and risk moderating its present ideological tendencies or to ignore and suppress the popular will, risking increasing social polarization and greater alienation between the government and population. Regardless of any preferences of Khamenei and the *nezam*'s current institutions, these pressures will almost certainly influence any longer-term context in which succession occurs.

Finally, relations between Iran and the United States could affect what follows Khamenei, should he continue to rule for many years. The ultimate outcome of the ongoing confrontation over Iran's nuclear program looms large in this relationship. But other issues like human rights, Iran's support for terrorism, and prospects for peace or continued conflict between Israel and its Palestinian and other Arab neighbors play pivotal roles as well. A "history" is yet to be written of this relationship over the next decade or so, and it too will inform a longer-term succession.

Acknowledgments

The authors wish to thank a number of people for their support of the research contained in this document. First, many thanks go to Richard Cappelli and Brendan Dillon for their guidance and insights as sponsors of the project. We would also like to thank John Parachini and Kathi Webb—director and associate director, respectively, of the RAND Intelligence Policy Center—for their encouragement and patient oversight of the study.

The authors would like to express great appreciation for the time and insights of a number of top Iran scholars in the United States and elsewhere, whose contributions were extremely valuable. Without them, this research would not have been possible. We engaged these scholars in very fruitful discussions about informal networks in Iran in an effort to gain greater understanding of the Iranian "system." Many of them prefer to remain anonymous because of the sensitive nature of their activities.

Barbara Sude of RAND and Steve Simon of the Council on Foreign Relations provided insightful and extremely helpful comments on the draft of this monograph. We conducted important organizational and substantive revisions on the basis of their thoughtful recommendations, and we are deeply indebted to them.

The authors offer profound gratitude to RAND colleague John Limbert, who offered sage advice based on his decades of Iran expertise and provided very helpful comments on our research. We also thank former RAND colleague Charlotte Lynch for collecting important documents and articles on the history of the Supreme Leader and the Islamic Republic.

Finally, the authors would like to thank RAND colleagues Patrice Lester and Francisco Walter for their help with citations and manuscript preparation and Nora Spiering and Erin Johnson for editing the manuscript.

Of course, the content of this report is the sole responsibility of the authors.

Abbreviations

IRP   Islamic Republic Party

SCC   Society of Combatant Clergymen

CHAPTER ONE

Introduction

The tumultuous 2009 presidential election shattered Iran's political equilibrium and riveted the international community. Only hours after the polls closed, the Interior Ministry announced that the incumbent, Mahmoud Ahmadinejad, had won by a landslide, with 63 percent of the vote.[1] Upon hearing the news, opposition groups alleged fraud, and millions of Iranians poured into the streets in protest. Not since the Islamic Revolution in 1979 had such massive demonstrations by people from all sectors of society swept across the nation. The Islamic Revolutionary Guards Corps and the Basij militia violently cracked down on the uprisings, killing dozens and arresting thousands of demonstrators. Yet even these extensive measures could not fully stem the tide: Mass protests continued for the next six months, culminating in the Ashura protests in December 2009. Only in February of 2010 was the government largely able to suppress public demonstrations.

At the center of the storm stood the Supreme Leader of the Islamic Republic, Ayatollah Ali Khamenei. As the highest political authority in Iran, he was responsible for overseeing the conduct of the elections. As commander in chief, he also ordered the government response to the protests, including the violent crackdown by the Revolutionary Guards and other security forces whose commanders he had appointed. And, having portrayed himself publicly throughout his 20-year rule as an even-handed "arbiter" between factions, above the political fray, he

---

[1]   Robert F. Worth and Nazila Fathi, "Protests Flare in Tehran as Opposition Disputes Vote," *New York Times*, June 13, 2009.

nevertheless decisively endorsed the hard-right bloc of Ahmadinejad's supporters.

The 2009 election was transformative for Iran. The unspoken contract between the government and the people—in which Iranians were permitted some political participation and limited personal space in return for acquiescence to the status quo—was shattered. The Islamist Left political grouping was effectively pushed out of the political system. The Revolutionary Guards emerged as the dominant political and economic institution in the country. Deep fractures among long-standing members of Iran's leadership and clergy, traditionally addressed in the Islamic Republic behind closed doors, were uncharacteristically aired in public, as key figures openly expressed their dismay at the government's handling of the election and subsequent protests. The country had taken an irrevocable turn.

Khamenei's central position as Supreme Leader affords him the capacity to broadly shape the overall direction of the Islamic Republic. In the 2009 election, he exercised that capacity definitively. He rules through a combination of considerable constitutional authority and informal paths of influence over key institutions and power centers. He plays a pivotal role in Iran's domestic policy, delineating "the general policies of the Islamic Republic" and supervising "the proper execution of [those] policies."[2] As seen in June 2009, he ratifies the electorate's choice of president. He directly appoints the principal decision-makers across many domains: senior state officials, the commanders of the Revolutionary Guards and the Artesh (Iran's conventional armed forces),[3] and the heads of the judiciary and the clerical jurists of the Guardian Council.[4] He decides on the management of Islamic Republic of Iran Broadcasting. The Supreme Leader also steers Iran's foreign

---

[2]   For a translation of the 1989 constitution, see Axel Tschentscher, ed., "Iran: Constitution," International Constitutional Law, 1995, Article 110.

[3]   For more on Iran's military, see Frederic Wehrey, David E. Thaler, Nora Bensahel, Kim Cragin, Jerrold D. Green, Dalia Dassa Kaye, Nadia Oweidat, and Jennifer Li, *Dangerous But Not Omnipotent: Exploring the Reach and Limitations of Iranian Power in the Middle East*, Santa Monica, Calif.: RAND Corporation, MG-781-AF, 2009b, pp. 39–80.

[4]   The Guardian Council, a traditionally conservative body, consists of 12 jurists (six clerical and six nonclerical). It reviews Majles (the Iranian parliament) legislation for adherence

policy and holds the key to relations with the outside world, especially the United States.

However, Ayatollah Khamenei will not serve as Supreme Leader forever. There have been persistent rumors about his health, including reports of cancer, although, at 71 years old, he may have many years ahead of him. Iran is one of the most important challenges to U.S. interests in the Middle East. A future Supreme Leader, if the institution persists, will affect U.S.-Iranian relations for better or ill. Consequently, it is critical for U.S. policymakers to begin preparing now for the future succession.

The Official Procedure for Selecting Iran's Supreme Leader Is Laid Out in the Iranian Constitution

The Iranian constitution specifies that the Supreme Leader is directly elected by the Assembly of Experts. Once elected, the Supreme Leader may remain in that position for life. After he takes office, the assembly is formally responsible for supervising his performance. It has the authority to declare him incompetent and, if need be, to remove him.[5]

The assembly is composed of 86 clerics and is required to convene twice a year. Technically, these clerics are elected by the Iranian people for eight-year terms. But all candidates for the assembly are also vetted by the 12-member Guardian Council. Six of the Guardian Council's members are appointed by the Supreme Leader; the rest are chosen by the Judiciary Chief, also appointed by the Supreme Leader. This gives the Supreme Leader effective control of the Guardian Council, which in turn, essentially allows him to control the Assembly of Experts. The Supreme Leader's influence within the constitutional process ensures the election of conservative and largely loyal members to the assembly.

The regime often cites the assembly's role in selecting the Supreme Leader as an example of the "democratic" nature of the office. How-

---

to sharia and the constitution and oversees all elections, including the vetting of candidates. See Tschentscher, 1995, Article 99.

[5]   See Tschentscher, 1995, Articles 107 and 111.

ever, the assembly's decisions and deliberations are largely confidential and not open to public scrutiny.

In Actuality, the Next Succession Is Likely to Occur in a Much Different Way

Despite being the cornerstone of the official constitutional procedure, the Assembly of Experts is, in fact, currently powerless to shape succession independently. The next succession—if there even is one after Khamenei leaves the scene—will most likely be determined in a more informal way. Assuming that Iran has not undergone major political changes before that time,[6] three principal factors will play a key role:

- the factional balance of power
- the dominant interpretation of *velayat-e faghih*—a foundational concept that justifies the political rule of the clergy in an Islamic state
- the interests of Khamenei's personal network.

The Factional Balance of Power

The Supreme Leader oversees a political system where "the informal trumps the formal . . . and domestic factional dynamics drive policy debates and policy making."[7] Factions in Iran are fluid politi-

---

[6]   The June 2009 election and the subsequent creation of the oppositionist Green Movement have demonstrated that seismic change within Iranian politics is possible, including the demise of the Islamic Republic. Should this happen, neither the informal nor the formal structures of the current system would shape succession.

[7]   David E. Thaler, Alireza Nader, Shahram Chubin, Jerrold D. Green, Charlotte Lynch, and Frederic Wehrey, *Mullahs, Guards, and* Bonyads: *An Exploration of Iranian Leadership Dynamics*, Santa Monica, Calif.: RAND Corporation, MG-878-OSD, 2010, p. xii. For other studies on Iran's political system and the role of the Supreme Leader, see also Wilfried Buchta, *Who Rules Iran? The Structure of Power in the Islamic Republic*, Washington, D.C.: The Washington Institute for Near East Policy and the Konrad-Adenauer-Stiftung, 2000; Karim Sadjadpour, *Reading Khamenei: The World View of Iran's Most Powerful Leader*, Washington, D.C.: Carnegie Endowment for International Peace, 2008; and Ray Takeyh, *Hidden Iran: Paradox and Power in the Islamic Republic*, New York: Times Books, 2006.

cal groupings of influential individuals, relationships, and power centers with compatible worldviews, policy preferences, and visions for the Islamic Republic. The bifurcated nature of the Iranian political system between theocracy and republicanism, and the influence of informal networks, create a dysfunctional decisionmaking system that is a breeding ground for intense, at times brutal, factional competition for power and influence.

Currently in Iran, there are two overarching factional groupings: the Islamist Left and the Islamist Right. Within those groupings are four key factions: reformists, pragmatic conservatives, traditional conservatives, and principlists.[8] The reformists are associated with the Islamist Left, while the other three factions fall within the Islamist Right.[9] Of the latter three, the pragmatic conservatives and traditional conservatives tend to be less ideological than the principlists, although ideology does play a substantial role in shaping the worldview of all of the factions.

All four factions share an interest in the continuation of the Islamic Republic and the Islamic Revolution; however, they have very different interpretations of those notions and very different visions of Iran's future. Generally, the Islamist Right sees Iran as a revolutionary state with conservative social mores and an assertive foreign policy. Conversely, the Islamist Left focuses on the *nezam*'s republican nature and advocates a less-restrictive, mainstream state that is more cooperative with the international community.

The shape of factional competition will be a decisive factor in the next succession for two primary reasons: First, since the Islamic Revolution in 1979, factionalism has been more important than constitutional process in determining who becomes Supreme Leader. It played a major role in the events that led to Khamenei succeeding Khomeini in 1989.

---

[8]   Identifying specific factions in the Islamic Republic is an art rather than a science. The four we name here were identified in Thaler et al., 2010, and Wehrey et al., 2009b.

[9]   It should be noted that there are divisions within the reformist camp, though the 2009 election and opposition to the status quo has been a unifying factor.

Second, factionalism has intensified markedly since Khamenei took power, and its influence on Iranian politics has grown steadily stronger over the past two decades. This trend shows no sign of abating. Consequently, it is very likely to play an even bigger role in the next succession than in 1989, with the four main Iranian factions maneuvering for advantage in the lead-up to Khamenei's departure.

The Prevailing View of *Velayat-e Faghih*

The concept of the *velayat-e faghih*, or "the rule of the supreme jurisprudent," forms the basis of the political system of the Islamic Republic of Iran as it exists today. *Velayat-e faghih* is an ideological notion with roots in Shi'a Islam that justifies the political rule of the clergy in an Islamic state. There have been different interpretations of the concept over its long history. The authority of the position of Supreme Leader today is based on Khomeini's interpretation. However, each of Iran's four factions has a particular interpretation of *velayat-e faghih*, each of which, in turn, points to a different view of the office of Supreme Leader. As the basis of Iran's political system, *velayat-e faghih* is the starting point for any discussion of Iranian politics—particularly for discussion of an issue as fundamental as the Supreme Leader. Given that it also helps define each of Iran's main factions, whose power struggle will be critical in the next succession, *velayat-e faghih* will, by extension, also play a pivotal role in shaping succession.

Khamenei's Personal Network

Over his time in office, Khamenei has created and strengthened his own personal network to ensure his authority within the Islamic Republic. This network is composed of a broad array of stakeholders:

- advisors and functionaries within the Supreme Leader's office
- the Supreme Leader's representatives in the armed forces and the security establishment, including key members of the Revolutionary Guards
- Friday prayer leaders
- other elites within key Iranian seminaries and clerical associations.

Khamenei's personal network is, first and foremost, loyal to him rather than to any one faction. Most members hail from the Islamist Right, but within that bloc, there are traditional conservatives, pragmatic conservatives, and pro- and anti-Ahmadinejad principlists. Loyalty to Khamenei and dependence on him for power and patronage tie these disparate factions and personalities together within the network.

There are two principal reasons why it appears very likely that Khamenei's personal network will have a determining say in the next succession. First, there is a strong historical precedent: Khomeini, too, maintained a personal network that exerted a significant influence over political decisionmaking in Iran, including the choice of his successor. Second, since the presidency of Mohammed Khatami (1997–2005), Khamenei and his personal network have assumed greater and greater authority, and they are now the primary decisionmakers in Iranian politics, superseding the country's formal political processes. As the next succession approaches, this network will want to retain its power and will make decisions based on its members' vested interests. Given its current degree of influence, those decisions will almost certainly carry significant weight.

Other Potential Factors Are Not as Relevant if the Succession Happens in the Near Term

Iran is in a state of great societal, religious, and political transformation. The Green Movement, the women's rights movement, Iran's declining economy, and its relations with the United States could all also play a role in determining the succession to the next Supreme Leader.

However, our focus is succession in the near term, as it would take place within the current political system—that is, within the next two to three years. The three factors we have identified as being the most important in shaping it are all defining elements of the Islamic Republic's political system as it exists today. The Green Movement, for instance, although still a prominent force in Iranian politics, is, at this time, politically marginalized and unlikely to be in a position to shape succession directly. It and other factors may indeed play some part in what happens in the next two to three years, but that part will be secondary in comparison with the impact of the three principal factors. Should the succession take place in the longer term—within a decade or two—a number of those other, currently marginal, factors may indeed come to assume a more decisive role.

The Trajectory of the Next Succession Will Hinge on How the Three Principal Factors Are Configured at the Time of Khamenei's Departure

How these three factors line up at the time of the next succession will have a tremendous impact on what follows after Khamenei departs the scene. These factors are by no means static; on the contrary, they are highly dynamic, evolving in response to societal pressures and political events. Accordingly, in combination they could lead to any number of succession scenarios, depending on how they stack up when the time for succession comes. By keeping track of how these factors are developing and reconfiguring over time, analysts and policymakers can assess the likelihood that the next succession will take a particular form. Here, indicators provide an invaluable tool. Indicators are associated with each of the three factors and serve as "anchor points" of sorts that can be observed to track how the factors are evolving in relation to each other, suggesting a trajectory toward a given scenario.

With this in mind, the objectives of our study are twofold: (1) to shed light on how the position and role of the Supreme Leader might change after Khamenei leaves the scene and (2) to point to indicators associated with the three key factors that are likely to provide insight into what form the next succession will take. We believe that analysts can benefit from first naming and then tracking indicators along the lines of those we identify here, as a means of evaluating what ongoing debate and activity within the Islamic Republic imply about the next Supreme Leader.

To demonstrate how this would work, we outline five possible scenarios and show how the three factors would need to evolve from the present time until the next succession (within the next three years) for any one of them to come to pass. We emphasize that our scenarios are not predictive (we have no confidence that Iran after Khamenei will look *exactly* like one of them). Rather, they are tools for analysis. The current configuration of factors does suggest that certain of our scenarios are more likely if the succession should take place in the near term, and we discuss that. But it is also possible that Khamenei will remain Supreme Leader for ten years or more. Consequently, we also speculate briefly about the changes that are likely to ensue in the longer term if Khamenei retains power beyond the next three years.

Methodology

We began our analysis with a comprehensive review of a wide range of primary and secondary open sources. These included Persian-language sources, such as governmental and nongovernmental (e.g., clerical) websites, official statements, and Iranian media reports. We also examined Ayatollah Khomeini's writings and the constitution of the Islamic Republic (adopted in 1979 and revised in 1989). To complement this review, we consulted with a number of experts on Iran outside of RAND, including Iranian academicians and former Iranian government officials. These interlocutors requested anonymity but were extremely helpful in framing and informing our research. Finally, we drew from numerous U.S. and European studies on Iranian domestic politics, particularly a sizeable group of recent RAND studies on Iran.[10]

---

[10] Thaler et al., 2010; Daniel Byman, Shahram Chubin, Anoushiravan Ehteshami, and Jerrold D. Green, *Iran's Security Policy in the Post-Revolutionary Era*, Santa Monica, Calif.: RAND Corporation, MR-1320-OSD, 2001; Wehrey et al., 2009b; Frederic Wehrey, Jerrold D. Green, Brian Nichiporuk, Alireza Nader, Lydia Hansell, Rasool Nafisi, and S. R. Bohandy, *The Rise of the Pasdaran: Assessing the Domestic Roles of the Islamic Revolutionary Guards Corps*, Santa Monica, Calif.: RAND Corporation, MG-821-OSD, 2009a; Jerrold D. Green, Frederic Wehrey, and Charles Wolf, Jr., *Understanding Iran*, Santa Monica, Calif.: RAND Corporation, MG-771-SRF, 2009; and Keith Crane, Rollie Lal, and Jeffrey Martini, *Iran's Political, Demographic, and Economic Vulnerabilities*, Santa Monica, Calif.: RAND Corporation, MG-693-AF, 2008.

Using these materials, we conducted a historical analysis of the institution of Supreme Leader and key aspects of Khomeini's and Khamenei's terms in the position. First studying the justifications for the creation of the Supreme Leader position during the Islamic Revolution, we then analyzed the position's constitutional and informal powers and Khomeini and Khamenei's uses of these powers. We also scrutinized various debates in Iran on the nature of the Supreme Leader, including those related to the 1989 succession.

On the basis of this extensive research, we identified the three primary factors that we believe will shape the next succession, if it happens in the near term, and the character of the next Supreme Leader (if there is one), along with associated indicators. We then developed the five scenarios.

Roadmap of the Report

Chapters Two, Three, and Four present the three key factors that will shape the next succession. Chapter Two explores the role of factional competition for power in Iran in the 1989 succession and its prevalence in Iranian politics today. Chapter Three deals with the concept of *velayat-e faqhih*. Chapter Four analyzes the importance of the personal network on which Khamenei relies to maintain his hold on power and influence and lead the direction of the Islamic Republic. We outline the five scenarios for succession in Chapter Five, mapping potential trajectories of succession by focusing on the indicators that can help U.S. and other observers assess and discuss how the three key factors are evolving. In Chapter Six, we first briefly discuss which of these scenarios is most likely given the current configuration of factors and then speculate about succession should it take place in the longer term. Finally, we offer a few words of conclusion in Chapter Seven.

CHAPTER TWO

Factor 1: The Factional Balance of Power

Factionalism has been a fixture of Iran's political system since the Islamic revolution of 1979. Over the ensuing three decades, various factions across the political spectrum have frequently taken advantage of Iran's relatively weak elected institutions to shape major policies. Indeed, factionalism has generally been more important than constitutional process in decisionmaking. While Khomeini was able to keep factionalism largely in check by providing a point of commonality that united the different factions, this has not been the case since Khamenei took power in 1989. Factional competition has grown markedly in both intensity and influence since that time and has arguably become the defining feature of the contemporary Iranian political system.

For both of these reasons, the factional "war" in Iran will be a decisive factor in the next succession. Khamenei's passing will be a critical juncture for the *nezam*'s factions, each of which has a deep and vested interest in shaping what follows him, and the future of Iran.

The Factional Landscape in Iran

The *nezam*'s factional landscape can broadly be divided into two factional groups, the Islamist Right and the Islamist Left. The Right is currently split into three factions: the traditional conservatives, the pragmatic conservatives, and the principlists (Figure 2.1).

All of the factions within these two broad groupings—both Right and Left—share certain common beliefs and objectives:

Figure 2.1
Factions in Iran on the Spectrum of Liberal to Conservative

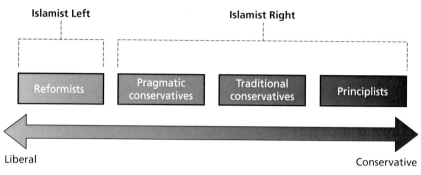

RAND *MG1052-2.1*

- All are devoted to Ayatollah Khomeini and the Islamic Revolution.
- All are committed to an Islamist system of government that excludes "nonrevolutionary" and secular parties.
- All agree that the Islamic Republic's fundamental security interest is the survival and strengthening of the *nezam*.

But beyond these commonalities, the four factions are quite distinct and vie for political power.

The Islamist Right

The Islamist Right has largely dominated Iran since Supreme Leader Khamenei took office in 1989. Many of its most prominent members—including Khamenei, Ayatollah Ali Akbar Hashemi Rafsanjani, and Ayatollah Ahmad Jannati—are part of the conservative clerical establishment that has ruled Iran for the past three decades. The Islamist Right is unified by a common vision of the revolution and the future of the Islamic Republic and has generally supported the political status quo. But, with three major factions, it is far from a monolithic force.

The Traditional Conservatives. The traditional conservatives are primarily members of the clerical elite who overthrew the Shah and established the Islamic Republic in 1979. They are considered to be the Islamic Republic's "old guard." They believe in the continuation of the Islamic Republic in its current form and a "traditional" Islamic society.

They endorse a foreign policy of "resistance" vis-à-vis the West and the United States.

The traditional conservatives draw support from the clergy in Qom, as well as the lower religious classes and the bazaar. They exercise their influence over politics via religious institutions and the seminaries and also through control of such powerful associations as the Association of Qom Seminary Teachers and the Society of Combatant Clergymen (SCC).

Typically loyal proponents of Khamenei's rule, they are vested in an Islamist system of government that perpetuates their power and influence. But certain traditional conservatives, including some senior clergymen, have demonstrated a willingness to criticize Khamenei for his authoritarian style of governance and unqualified support for Ahmadinejad during the 2009 presidential election.

The Pragmatic Conservatives. The pragmatic conservatives are the most "liberal" of the three factions within the Islamist Right. They largely share the traditional conservatives' views on religion and Islamic society, but they differ on economic and foreign policy. The pragmatic conservative faction is particularly concerned about the continued viability of the Islamic Republic as a political and economic system. In this sense, its members favor Iran's modernization and relatively greater cooperation with the international community—especially the West and possibly the United States. While they do not often advocate wide-scale political reforms, they realize that some reforms on the political front may be needed to achieve what they see as necessary economic reforms. Many would prefer the Chinese model of economic progress without extensive democratization.

The pragmatic conservatives garner strong support from Iranian technocrats and the government bureaucracy. They have also drawn the backing of segments of Iran's merchant and business classes. Rafsanjani, current chief of the Expediency Council and the Assembly of Experts, can be considered the dean of the pragmatic conservative faction. As president of the Islamic Republic from 1989 to 1997, Rafsanjani pursued economic privatization in Iran in tandem with warmer relations with regional Arab states and leading European countries. Under

Rafsanjani, Iran began to move away from some of its more radical policies, such as the export of the revolution to Arab countries.

The Principlists. The principlists are the most ideological of the Islamist Right factions, calling for a "return" to the principles of the Islamic Revolution. In contrast to the traditional conservatives, the principlists represent the "new guard" of the Islamic Republic. They view the revolution—and, by extension, the Islamic Republic—as an ideal that should not be subjected to reforms. Accordingly, they favor domestic policies that emphasize "social justice," redistribution of wealth, and austere societal norms and personal conduct. In terms of foreign policy, the principlists follow the revolutionary creed of resistance to Western "imperialism." They tend to view the United States in ideological terms and are less prone to compromise or negotiate on such issues as the Iranian nuclear program. They view reformists and even the pragmatic conservatives—in short, anyone who advocates fundamental change within the *nezam*—as a danger to the revolution and the Islamic Republic.

The principlists are currently the most powerful faction within the Iranian government. They are primarily associated with the Ahmadinejad administration and the rise of the Revolutionary Guards within Iranian politics.[1] Many hail from either the Guards or the paramilitary Basij and have been shaped by their experiences of the Iran-Iraq War. President Ahmadinejad and his religious mentor, Ayatollah Mesbah-Yazdi, are key figures within the principlist faction.

Like the traditional conservatives, the principlists favor an Islamist society ruled according to religious law and appear to be highly loyal to Khamenei as Supreme Leader. Nevertheless, elements of the principlists' ideology are shaped by anticlerical beliefs, which set them apart from the traditional conservatives. Ahmadinejad and his close associates, for example, are Mahdists or millenarians, who are rumored to be tied to the secretive and anticlerical Hojjatieh society. Mahdists, such as Ahmadinejad, emphasize a personal connection with the Mahdi, or Hidden Imam. This is a position quite different from that taken by tra-

---

[1]   It should be noted that there are deep cleavages within the principlist camp, especially in regard to Ahmadinejad's leadership abilities.

ditional conservatives, who view the clergy as spiritual intermediaries between the masses and the Mahdi. In practical terms, this means that the principlists, though largely loyal to Khamenei, consider the clergy to be less relevant in governing the Islamic Republic.

The Islamist Left (Reformists)

The Islamist Left is primarily composed of "reformed" revolutionaries, intellectuals, civil rights activists, and students. Its members have increasingly questioned the legitimacy and efficacy of Iran's current system of governance, especially regarding the Supreme Leader's role. They contend that a strong civil society will maintain individual rights while preserving the religious characteristics of the Islamic Republic. Women and ethnic minorities have been relatively supportive of the Islamist Left.

The Islamist Left is primarily associated with leading opposition figures, such as the main losing candidate in the 2009 presidential elections, former Prime Minister Mir Hussein Mousavi. The Islamist Left is broadly represented in the Green Movement, a grass-roots opposition movement that formed in the immediate aftermath of Ahmadinejad's reelection. Ostensibly centered around Mousavi, the Green Movement is an extensive network of reformist groups and other sectors of Iranian society, especially the young, who are opposed not only to Ahmadinejad's reelection but to the political status quo as a whole. There are points of divergence within the Islamist Left, as well as rivalries. Mousavi, former speaker of parliament Mehdi Karroubi, and Khatami are united in challenging what they view as an illegitimate government but do not appear to share a common set of ultimate objectives. Yet these differences are not pronounced enough to have formed a basis for discernably separate factions within the Islamist Left, so it is treated here as a unified group.

Since the Islamic Revolution, Factionalism Has Been More Influential Than Constitutional Process in Decisionmaking and Policymaking Within the Iranian Political System

The Islamic Republic's political system may be defined by the constitution, but factional politics are one of the most influential of factors shaping politics in Iran since the revolution. For example, the power of the president is well defined by the constitution, but the power of each president has been determined by his factional affiliation and the Supreme Leader's preferences. Khatami was often powerless to shape domestic and foreign policies because of his reformist inclinations, whereas Rafsanjani and Ahmadinejad have exercised significant power. The influence of factionalism on politics may have reached its apogee in the 2009 presidential election, in which Ahmadinejad's factional affiliation and Khamenei's support for him ensured his electoral victory, rather than the vote of the electorate.

The role of the Assembly of Experts demonstrates the influence of factionalism in elite politics. The assembly has the authority to select and supervise the next Supreme Leader. In reality, factional jockeying determined the assembly's decision regarding the Supreme Leader in 1989 much more than constitutional procedures did. The Islamist Right faction that dominated the assembly determined the assembly's actions in the 1989 succession according to its own narrow interests. The assembly obeyed Khomeini's orders by revising the constitution to allow Khamenei to be selected as Supreme Leader without independent deliberation.

In essence, the assembly acted as a "rubber stamp" body rather than a fully empowered government institution. It was largely compliant during Khomeini's leadership and has not performed a supervisory role under Khamenei. This is due to the fact that much of the assembly of 86 clerics has been dominated by traditional conservatives who have tended to support *velayat-e faghih*.[2]

---

[2]   Ayatollah Ali Meshkini was chief of the assembly for more than 20 years, from 1984 to 2007. One of the founding fathers of the Islamic Republic, he was a firm supporter of the Islamist Right. Meshkini was a devoted supporter of Khomeini's *velayat-e faghih* who saw little need for direct assembly intervention in the Supreme Leader's affairs.

Khomeini Was Able to Keep Factional Jockeying Largely in Check

Factional competition existed during Khomeini's rule, but the degree to which it had an influence in shaping politics was limited. Khomeini's tremendous authority and stature as the father of the Islamic Revolution and founder of the Islamic Republic provided a point of commonality that united all of the different groups within the system. During his reign as Supreme Leader, Khomeini limited the effects of factional competition by staying above the fray: He never explicitly identified himself as linked to any particular faction. These actions ensured a wide and faithful following among the *nezam*'s feuding elite until his death. In fact, the Islamist Left was perhaps the most devoted bastion of support for Khomeini and his revolutionary cause. Mir Hussein Mousavi was Khomeini's loyal prime minister in the 1980s and remains devoted to his vision and ideology today.

Khomeini's ability to unify Iran's factions allowed him to designate his successor without much factional opposition. The Islamist Left respected Khomeini's authority to such an extent that it did not seriously challenge his selection of Khamenei, a low-ranking cleric. But Khomeini's choice of Khamenei actually turned out to be far more beneficial for the Islamist Right.

Traditional conservatives of the time, such as Khamenei and Rafsanjani, although well suited ideologically for leadership roles, lacked the charisma, experience, and religious standing to assume the position of Supreme Leader. Moreover, the 1979 constitution stipulated that the Supreme Leader be "recognized and accepted as *marja* and leader by a decisive majority of the people."[3] Only a few clergymen in Iran were widely recognized *marjas* (sources of emulation) at the time of succession, and some were not even devoted followers of Khomeini's conception of *velayat-e faghih*, presenting a significant challenge to his plans for succession. He asked the Assembly of Experts to revise the 1979 constitution. The *marja* clause was eliminated, and Khamenei

---

[3]   Hamid Algar, trans., *Constitution of the Islamic Republic of Iran*, Berkeley, Calif.: Mizan Press, 1980a.

was confirmed by the Assembly of Experts as Khomeini's successor. His succession carried risks, particularly given his lack of religious credentials, yet it fulfilled the needs of the dominant conservative faction centered around Khomeini and his personal network.

Since Khamenei Came to Power in 1989, Factional Competition Has Grown Markedly in Both Intensity and Influence

Khomeini's death led to increased factionalism, which has become a much more significant factor in Iranian politics since that time. Khamenei has been greatly responsible for the *nezam*'s growing factionalism. During the first few years of his leadership, he followed more "moderate" or even pragmatic conservative Islamist Right policies, as he lacked Khomeini's iconic status and an independent political network, and was reliant on more pragmatic conservative figures, such as Rafsanjani, who had in many ways been Khomeini's right-hand man.

But Khamenei's growing power as Supreme Leader over time allowed him to shift away from the pragmatic Islamist Right. Khamenei made perhaps his first public criticism of Rafsanjani and the pragmatic trend in Iranian politics in 1992, when he stated that "some [in the system] mock the Hizbollahis and their religious virtues, but if we spend billions on development projects and ignore moral issues in the country, all their achievements amount to nothing."[4]

Khamenei, who appears to have been much more conservative than Rafsanjani to begin with, may have felt that his consolidation of power as Supreme Leader provided an opportunity to shift more to the right of the political spectrum. In addition, he began to feel a growing threat to *velayat-e faghih* and his authority as Supreme Leader in the mid-1990s. The challenge to his authority emanated from the pragmatic elements of the Islamist Right—especially the technocrats

---

[4]   Mehdi Moslem, *Factional Politics in Post-Khomeini Iran*, Syracuse, N.Y.: Syracuse University Press, 2002, p. 201.

organized around Rafsanjani and such pragmatic conservative groups as the *Kargozaran-e Sazandegi* (Executives of Construction).

But the Islamist Left and the reformists posed even a bigger challenge to him after Khatami was elected president in 1997. Some of the reformists viewed *velayat-e faghih* and the institution of the Supreme Leader as the main impediments to much-needed social, economic, and political reforms. In reaction, Khamenei increasingly supported the extreme wing of the Islamist Right, including principlist elements in the Revolutionary Guards and the Basij.

Khamenei's support of the principlists may have strengthened his hand as Supreme Leader, but it also created great tension within the *nezam*. The Islamist Left, though devoted to Khomeini and his revolutionary cause, saw its influence wane under the leadership of Ayatollah Khamenei. The Islamist Left's exclusion from the center of power under Khamenei has caused it to become more critical of the institution of the Supreme Leader.

The post-2009 crisis affecting the Islamic Republic has been the result of increased factionalism under Khamenei's leadership. Whereas Khomeini kept various factions under the same tent, so to speak, Khamenei's support of a narrow section of the principlists has upset the *nezam*'s factional equilibrium. Today, the Islamic Republic is increasingly a militarized and authoritarian system of government that excludes factions and personalities that were once the bedrock of the revolutionary state. The Islamic Republic's political exclusiveness may strengthen Khamenei's hand in the short term and determine succession in the near term. Yet it may cause long-term instability for the *nezam* and perhaps its ultimate demise.

CHAPTER THREE

Factor 2: The Prevailing View of *Velayat-e Faghih*

Velayat-e faghih has served as the foundation of the Islamic Republic of Iran for over three decades. It is the source from which the Supreme Leader derives legitimacy for his simultaneous political and religious authority over the country. The roots of *velayat-e faghih* lie in Shi'a Islam. For much of Shi'a Iran's history,[1] *velayat-e faghih* justified the clergy's temporal guardianship of a narrow section of the population: the weak, orphaned, and infirm—individuals considered to be vulnerable members of society, unprotected by the state. Under this doctrine, a ranking member of the clergy, usually a *marja-e taghlid* (source of emulation), would have the authority to assume not only religious but also temporal guardianship of this community.

In the years leading up to the Islamic Revolution, Ayatollah Khomeini reconceptualized *velayat-e faghih* to justify the new Islamic state that replaced the Shah in 1979. Although the traditional concept of *velayat-e faghih* had entailed a very narrow definition of clerical guardianship, it gave the widely venerated Khomeini enough to build on to establish the necessary religious justification for his own political purposes. It is Khomeini's concept of *velayat-e faghih* that allows direct clerical involvement in Iranian state matters today.

In his 1970 book *Hokumat-e Islami* [*Islamic Government*], Khomeini stated:

---

[1]   Iran officially became a Shi'a state under the rule of the Safavid Dynasty in the 16th century.

Islamic government does not correspond to any of the existing forms of government. . . . [T]he fundamental difference between Islamic government, on the one hand, and constitutional monarchies and republics, on the other hand, is this: whereas representatives of the people or the monarch in such *nezams* engage in legislation, in Islam, legislative power and competence to establish laws belongs exclusively to God Almighty. The Sacred Legislator of Islam is the sole legislative power.[2]

Here Khomeini lays out his conception of an Islamic government based on a *velayat-e faghih* that supersedes the traditional Shi'a concept and excludes democratic norms. Significantly, Khomeini downplays constitutional rights in favor of "divine laws," thus putting in place the framework for a republic in which the people's political rights are subsumed under Islamic laws.

Since the revolution, multiple interpretations of *velayat-e faghih* have emerged. Currently, three main readings dominate discourse and decisionmaking in the Islamic Republic:

- Those who believe in *velayat-e faghih* as reconceptualized by Khomeini tend to endorse one of two interpretations—either the "absolute" or the "democratic."
- The "quietist" *velayat-e faghih* is closely aligned with the traditional concept.

Each reading of this core concept has a particular vision of what the Supreme Leader should look like, and each consequently implies a different possible future.

Velayat-e faghih will be an important factor in determining what happens in the next succession for several reasons. First, it is the ideological foundation of all politics in the Islamic Republic, enshrined in the Iranian constitution: Iran's highest ruler must by law be a religious authority. Khamenei's influence as the current Supreme Leader is heavily dependent on Khomeini's interpretation of *velayat-e faghih*. His

---

[2]   Hamid Algar, trans., *Islam and Revolution: Writings and Declarations of Imam Khomeini*, Berkeley, Calif.: Mizan Press, 1980b, p. 55.

power would be greatly weakened without a religious justification for his supreme political authority within a republican and representative (at least in name) political system. In a sense, *velayat-e faghih* is the glue that holds the position of the Supreme Leader onto the complex and at times "balkanized" Iranian *nezam*.

Second, with Khamenei's passing, the competition between these three views on *velayat-e faghih* is likely to intensify. Because the *nezam*'s various factions favor opposing interpretations of *velayat-e faghih*, a surge in factional competition before the next succession will also spark more-rigorous debate on the issue. Which interpretation of *velayat-e faghih* dominates the Islamic Republic, and the Assembly of Experts, during the succession process will help determine what happens after Khamenei's passing.

The Absolute View of *Velayat-e Faghih*

Proponents of *velayat-e motlagh-e faghih* (absolute rule of the supreme jurisprudent) believe that only the Supreme Leader, and not the republic's elected institutions, has the absolute right to make decisions for the state. According to this interpretation of the concept, the Supreme Leader's authority is divinely ordained, and he rules over the masses as the regent and representative of the Hidden Imam on earth. This authority is in no way based on popular will. In the most extreme version of this interpretation, the Supreme Leader holds the exclusive authority to govern, and such concepts as democracy and electoral politics are considered irrelevant, in light of his divine mandate. The state's political legitimacy is believed to be derived directly from God, who alone can create laws.

Velayat-e motlagh-e faghih is strongly supported by the far Islamist Right, including conservative clerical associations, such as the SCC; "principlist" political factions; and vigilante groups, such as the Ansar-e Hezbollah. They believe this version of the *velayat-e faghih*—advocated by Ayatollah Khamenei—to be the only legitimate and suitable system of rule for the Islamic Republic. They hold closely to what they consider to be Khomeini's view on *velayat-e faghih*. This means that any questioning of the concept—either from the quietists or the Islamist Left (or even conceivably from the Right)—is tantamount to betraying Khomeini and the Islamic Revolution.

Khomeini himself endorsed the absolute nature of *velayat-e faghih* toward the end of his life: In a 1988 decree, he stated that the Supreme Leader had near absolute powers.[3] The revised constitution of 1989 did much to reinforce the absolutist concept as well by prefacing the name of the Supreme Leader with the term *motlagh*.[4]

The principlist Ayatollah Mesbah-Yazdi is perhaps the most prominent and vocal proponent of absolute *velayat-e faghih* today. In Mesbah-Yazdi's eyes, the Supreme Leader's position is not bound by earthly laws and institutions. Consequently, his authority and decisions trump all other sources of state authority and override the *nezam*'s republican institutions, such as the parliament and the presidency. According to Mesbah-Yazdi, "neither the laws nor the officials of the state have any legitimacy unless and until they meet with the *vali e faghih's* [Supreme Leader's] approval."[5] Mesbah-Yazdi and the principlists discount the people's role in the political system, believing that they would become "infidels without the clergy."[6] In their view, the Supreme Leader, as guardian of the people, should be authorized to make decisions with or without their participation in the political system.

---

[3]   Moslem, 2002, p. 14.

[4]   Tschentscher, 1995, Article 57, reads: "The powers of government in the Islamic Republic are vested in the legislature, the judiciary, and the executive powers, functioning under the supervision of the *absolute* religious Leader and the Leadership of the Ummah, in accordance with the forthcoming articles of this Constitution. These powers are independent of each other."

[5]   Mehran Kamrava, *Iran's Intellectual Revolution*, Cambridge, England: Cambridge University Press, 2008, p. 105.

[6]   Ayatollah Mesbah-Yazdi, "Rouhaniyat Naboud, Mardom Kafer Mishodand ["Without the Clergy, the People Would Become Infidels]," Entekhab News, March 4, 2009.

The Democratic View of *Velayat-e Faghih*

Proponents of a democratic *velayat-e faghih* accept Khomeini's justification for clerical rule over an Islamic state. But they believe that instead of legitimizing an increasingly authoritarian decisionmaking system dominated by the Supreme Leader and the Revolutionary Guards, the concept of *velayat-e faghih* should include political decisionmaking by a broader section of the clergy and even the population. In this interpretation of the concept, the Supreme Leader's authority is both divinely ordained *and* popularly mandated. Popular will and electoral politics are seen as essential components of government in the Islamic Republic. The Supreme Leader must be accountable to the people and their elected representatives.

The notion of a democratic *velayat-e faghih* emerged among the intellectuals and activists of the reformist movement aligned with former President Khatami and such Islamist Left groups as the *Islamic Iran Participation Front* (*Jebheye Mosharekate Iran-e Islami*).[7] The Islamist Left believes that the *velayat-e faghih*, as conceptualized by Khomeini, is a valid and worthy system but feels that it has been applied incorrectly since Khomeini's passing. In the Islamist Left's view, *velayat-e faghih* does not translate into the absolute rule of just one person but should be a collective or representative responsibility. Mohsen Kadivar, a prominent reformist cleric residing in exile, offers an example of this thinking: "Article 56 of our constitution includes the right of God that is given to all Iranian citizens. The citizens then elect their leader, president and parliament. . . . [T]he leader must be elected and not selected by those claiming to know God's will."[8]

Ayatollah Hossein Ali Montazeri (1922–2009), one of Iran's leading *marjas,* Khomeini's original successor, and a prominent reformist, was the most preeminent advocate of democratic *velayat-e faghih*.

---

[7]   The democratic *velayat-e faghih* is not restricted to the Islamist Left. Certain elements of the Islamist Right—including pragmatic conservatives under Rafsanjani—have also discussed reforming the institution of the Supreme Leader and have even publicly discussed the creation of a Leadership Council among the *marja*.

[8]   Mohsen Kadivar, "This Iranian Form of Theocracy Has Failed," Spiegel Online, July 7, 2001.

According to Montazeri, the Supreme Leader should be subject to popular will through elections, term limits, and direct supervision by the Assembly of Experts:

> Although some of the *'ulama'* [clergy] are of the opinion that the position of *vali-e faqih* derives its authority from general appointment (*entesab-e 'amm*) by the infallible Imams . . . such opinions and their logic are subject to dispute and questioning. What is certain is that the external actualization and legitimacy of this position is rooted in its election by the nation; and in fact it is a social contract between the nation and *vali-e faqih*, and as such it is subject to the logic of faithfulness to agreements and covenants.[9]

Montazeri believed that the Supreme Leader should concern himself primarily with maintaining the *nezam*'s Islamic legitimacy rather than getting involved with day-to-day government. He viewed the Supreme Leader as a religious-ideological guardian, rather than the state's chief political executive. He advocated that this role should be formalized in the constitution by a clear statement mandating that the Supreme Leader be a *marja-e taghlid*.

Montazeri and other proponents of the democratic *velayat-e faghih* thought that the Supreme Leader should govern according to the Islamic concepts of *shura* (consultation)—that is, he should "rule" with the consensus of Iran's religious hierarchy:

> "[The *marjas*] will elect one person from among themselves for the general supervision of the process of running the country for a specific period of time, and he will be identified as the official *vali-e faqih*. Or alternatively, they may nominate more than one person so that the people could elect one of them as the *vali-e faghih* in a popular voting procedure. And it is most appropriate that arrangements are made so that the *maraje'* and the people could exercise supervision over the conduct of the *vali-e faghih*, and that he should be held accountable before the people."[10]

---

[9]   Geneive Abdo, "Re-Thinking the Islamic Republic: A Conversation with Ayatollah Hossein Ali Montazeri," *Middle East Journal*, Winter 2001.

[10]   Abdo, 2001.

This perspective suggests an executive body more akin to a Leadership Council, which has been intermittently proposed as an alternative to a single Supreme Leader over the Islamic Republic's three-decade history.

The Quietist View of *Velayat-e Faghih*

The quietist view of *velayat-e faghih* represents the Shi'a sect's traditional take on clerical participation in politics, which dominated Shi'a discourse on issues of religion and governance for centuries before the Islamic Revolution. Today, many quietists dominate Shi'a centers of thought outside of Iran in Najaf and Karbala and have influence in the Iranian holy city of Qom. This reading of *velayat-e faghih* is directly opposed to Khomeini's, centering on a relatively strict separation of religious and political matters. Those who hold the quietist view question the notion that *velayat-e faghih* provides a religious justification for clerical rule.

Over the past three decades, the Islamic Republic has been quite successful in enforcing Khomeini's view of *velayat-e faghih*. Accordingly, much of the political, if not intellectual discourse on *velayat-e faghih* has tended to stay within the *nezam*'s "red lines": Few have dared to challenge Khomeini's version of the concept publicly. Although a handful of Iranian thinkers and activists have questioned the need for a Supreme Leader, Iran's mainline political factions have accepted *velayat-e faghih* as a legitimate concept, even if some consider it in need of reform. As a result, the quietist view of *velayat-e faghih* has not enjoyed official sanction and has not been considered an effective alternative to the status quo.

But a sizeable group of clerics has continued to resist Khomeini's idea of *velayat-e faghih*. Despite three decades of Khomeinist rule in Iran, Qom today continues to be a source of quietism. It is unclear whether the majority of Iranian *marjas* and ayatollahs adhere to this traditional view of *velayat-e faghih*. The quietists in Qom have tended to express their views in private, if at all. *Marjas* in Qom who tend to avoid politics can provisionally be viewed as being anti–*velayat-e faghih*, but it is quite difficult to define any one *marja*'s political leanings.

Since Each Faction Has a Different View of *Velayat-e Faghih*, Whichever Dominates Iran's Political Landscape Will Play a Decisive Role in Shaping Succession

The Islamic Republic's traditional conservatives largely favor the status quo, though many appear concerned about Khamenei's increasingly authoritarian rule. The pragmatic conservatives, though loyal to the ideology of *velayat-e faghih*, favor a less authoritarian political system that does not preclude their active participation in decisionmaking, as has largely been the case under the Ahmadinejad administration, especially so after the 2009 election. Many pragmatic conservatives also appear to be opposed to the absolute version of *velayat-e faghih* and may be dissatisfied with Khamenei's style of politics. Thus, the pragmatic conservatives may favor a future institution of Supreme Leader that allows them greater participation in the political system and facilitates the implementation of their economic agenda.[11]

Rafsanjani has discussed reforming the system of *velayat-e faghih* and the institution of Supreme Leader. In a December 2008 speech, Rafsanjani proposed a "Fatwa Council" made up of Iran's *marjas*.[12] Though not strictly a Leadership Council, Rafsanjani's proposal resembles a system of government based on collective decisionmaking by the clergy. He has also advocated reforming Shi'a jurisprudence (*ijtehad*) in order to meet society's modern needs. According to Rafsanjani, "[T]here is a general consensus among all religious modernizers in Iran—whether of the reformist, pragmatist, or even fundamentalist variety—that we are at an important juncture, that we should keep up theologically with the times, or we run the risk of losing the masses of the faithful to secularizing tendencies and pressures."[13] Rafsanjani has indicated that the *nezam*'s current ideology of *velayat-e faghih* is not

---

[11] Khamenei was also chosen due to his ideological affinity with Khomeini and supporters of *velayat-e faghih* within the Islamist Right. Khomeini may have viewed Khamenei as being the most willing to pursue his legacy of *velayat-e faghih*, whereas such figures as Rafsanjani showed a more pragmatist streak on the subject.

[12] Kamal Nazer Yasin, "Iran: Rafsanjani at Center of Effort to Promote Reformation of Sh'ia Islam," EurasiaNet, January 30, 2009.

[13] Yasin, 2009.

necessarily compatible with the needs of a modern nation. Although a firm believer in the Islamic Revolution, Rafsanjani has nevertheless expressed his fear that the Islamic Republic faces significant dangers in the near future. His views on *ijtehad* and *velayat-e faghih* are widely reflected within the ideology of the "modern" Islamist Right, including such groups as the *Kargozaran-e Sazandegi*, which favors a more circumscribed role for the Supreme Leader.[14]

Other pragmatic conservatives, such as former national security advisor and Rafsanjani ally Hassan Rouhani, have not criticized the system of *velayat-e faghih* and Supreme Leader directly but have accused their opponents, namely Ahmadinejad, of "placing" the institution of the Supreme Leader as an obstacle "to freedom of speech and a free society."[15]

The reformists are somewhat in line with the pragmatic conservatives on the issue of the Supreme Leader, though they tend to favor a more democratic and inclusive institution of the Supreme Leader. The presidency of Mohammad Khatami from 1997–2005 and the flowering of the reformist movement revealed deep opposition to *velayat-e faghih* as practiced by Khamenei and supported by the Islamist Right. Reformist-minded clergymen, such as Montazeri and Kadivar, epitomize the Islamist Left view of *velayat-e faghih*, though it is not clear if they have in mind the exact and ideal shape of the office of Supreme Leader. In addition, such prominent figures as Khatami and former parliamentary speaker Mehdi Karroubi are careful not to cross the boundaries regarding *velayat-e faghih*. Campaigning for the 2009 presidential election, Karroubi clearly stated that "my red line is the *nezam*, Imam [meaning Khomeini], and the Supreme Leadership."[16]

---

[14] Moslem, 2002, p. 131.

[15] "Rouhani: Jafay e Bozorg Hamiyan Dolat be Rahbar e Enghelab" [Rouhani: Government Supporters' Greatest Unkindness Toward the Leader of the Revolution], Entekhab News, 2008.

[16] "Khat Ghermez man Nezam, Imam, va Rahbari Ast" [My Red Line is the Nezam, Imam, and the Supreme Leadership], Fars News Agency, April 10, 2009.

Nevertheless, the 2009 presidential election and the militarization of Iranian politics may have led such figures as Kadivar and perhaps even Karroubi to question the necessity of a Supreme Leader.

CHAPTER FOUR

Factor 3: Khamenei's Personal Network

Khamenei has taken advantage of Iran's informal and often inchoate political system to cement his personal power and authority at the expense of the *nezam*'s various decisionmaking bodies. He has accomplished this by cultivating a personal network loyal to him instead of to Iran's elected institutions. In return for loyalty, its members receive political and financial gains. This personal network serves as his "eyes and ears" and works in tandem with—or even in opposition to—Iran's three official branches of government. It allows him to definitively shape Iran's domestic and foreign policies despite the opposition of various factions and power centers. At the same time, it has increasingly enabled him to solidify the conservative ideology that shapes the current political status quo.

Some members of Khamenei's personal network hold official positions in the Iranian government. Others dominate key informal religious, clerical, and bazaari associations that serve as pillars of the Islamic Republic and the absolute *velayat-e faghih*. This network is not unprecedented in the history of the Islamic Republic: Khomeini, too, had an influential personal network, with some members working formally in the government and others holding informal positions throughout Iranian society. In keeping with his image as an arbiter standing above the factional fray, Khomeini populated his network with individuals from across the factional spectrum. Khomeini's personal network allowed him, in effect, to administer the Islamic Republic on the basis of his authority and ideology.

But what Khamenei has done with his network is quite different. Early in his rule, it was composed, like Khomeini's, of individuals and organizations with varying ideological and factional affiliations. But unlike Khomeini's, it was not very strong at the outset. Lacking the iconic stature and credentials of his predecessor, Khamenei began to encounter challenges to his authority quite soon after taking office. These scaled up markedly in the late 1990s when the reformist cleric Mohammed Khatami became president. To strengthen his position against this threat, Khamenei began to populate his personal network with a growing number of figures from the far Islamist Right and the principlist faction. At the same time, he started to push out reformists and pragmatic conservatives who had been part of his network early on. Gradually, Khamenei's personal network and his factional preference fused. This process began peaking in 2005 with the election of principlist Mohammed Ahmadinejad as president. It became definitive with the 2009 presidential election: At that point, Khamenei gave his personal network an unmistakable factional identity, and the narrowing of factional influence over national decisionmaking that had been taking place for the past several years or so became complete.

For all of these reasons, the tight-knit group that now dominates Khamenei's personal network will undoubtedly play a major role in the next succession. After he departs the scene, they will want to make sure that a similar patron succeeds him to ensure their positions within the *nezam*. The fact that his personal network has become factionalized will only strengthen that determination, as well as the degree of influence over what happens after Khamenei departs.

The Members of Khamenei's Personal Network

Khamenei's personal network currently includes:

Official advisors and government functionaries. These individuals work in the Office of the Supreme Leader and advisory bodies, such as the Strategic Council for Foreign Relations (*Shora-yi Rahbordi-yi Ravabet-i Khareji*).

Elements of the Revolutionary Guards. Principlists, such as Guards Commander in Chief Brigadier General Ali Jaffari, General Mohammad Hejazi (former chief of the Basij and chief of the Guards' joint staff), Hossein Taeb (current head of the Guards' intelligence organization), and several other high- and mid-ranking commanders are some of the leading members of Khamenei's personal network. The Guards' Political Bureau—responsible for enforcing revolutionary "principles" and the *velayat-e faghih* within the Guards—appears to serve as an important policy conduit between the Supreme Leader's office and the Guards' top brass.

The Basij forces. The paramilitary Basij forces are another important pillar of Khamenei's personal network. The Basij, which largely functioned as an auxiliary force for the Revolutionary Guards during the Iran-Iraq War, was formally incorporated into the Guards under General Jaffari's command in 2007.[1] It has today become a nationwide ideological militia of a "million" members also involved in economic, educational, and indoctrination activities. It has been given great leeway to operate as an enforcer of absolute *velayat-e faghih* and the political status quo.

Friday prayer leaders and clerical representatives. These clerics are appointed by Khamenei to lead Friday prayers throughout Iran. This group also includes Khamenei's representatives in religious seminaries and associations.

Key members of the *nezam*'s elite. Examples are parliamentary speaker Ali Larijani, former Minister of Foreign Affairs Ali Velayati, and former chief of the Revolutionary Guards Yahya Rahim Safavi.

Bonyads. Khamenei maintains indirect control of Iran's *bonyads* (foundations), which dominate much of Iran's economic activity. For example, he appoints the directors of some of the major *bonyads*, gaining access to a wide web of patronage and funding beyond state jurisdiction. These *bonyads* form an important part of his personal network. The Imam Reza Shrine Foundation in Mashhad, one of the largest business enterprises and landowners in Iran, is a prominent example.

---

[1]   Ali Alfoneh, "What Do Structural Changes in the Guards Mean?" American Enterprise Institute, September 2008.

The head of the foundation, Ayatollah Abbas Vaez Tabasi, has been a strong supporter of Khamenei and the absolutist reading of *velayat-e faghih*. He reportedly played an important role in Khamenei's selection as Supreme Leader by helping to block the creation of a Leadership Council.[2] In return, Khamenei has shown him support, from which he has benefited substantially. Tabasi is considered by some to be even more powerful than the official governor of Khorasan, the province where Mashhad is located.

Family members. Khamenei's son, Mojtaba, is reported to be an influential member of his father's personal network, serving as a conduit between Khamenei and the top echelon of the Revolutionary Guards and the Basij.[3] This would fit a well-established pattern in the Shi'a clerical community, where the oldest or most-trusted son often becomes his father's deputy or right-hand man. Khomeini's younger son, Ahmad, played a similar role for his father.

The Supreme Leader Has Historically Maintained a Personal Network Instrumental in Making Key Political Decisions

Iran has a long history of informal and often opaque decisionmaking. The modern Iranian state has lacked the type of procedural and legalistic system of government found in many advanced democracies. Prior to the Islamic Revolution, the strongman, quite often the reigning Shah, tended to make important state decisions behind closed doors, out of the public's view. He typically surrounded himself with a loyal informal personal network that played a key role in shaping policy and enforcing his authority.

Khomeini continued this tradition of an informal network that superseded the formal system of governance. He himself could not

---

[2] Mehdi Khalaji, *Apocalyptic Politics: On the Rationality of Iranian Policy*, Washington, D.C.: The Washington Institute for Near East Policy, January 2008.

[3] Julian Borger, "Mojtaba Khamenei: Gatekeeper to Iran's Supreme Leader," *The Guardian* (London), June 22, 2009.

have come to power without the active support of just such a network. After the revolution, a broad cross section of the opposition to the Shah contested Khomeini's strict vision of Islamist rule. But Khomeini managed to bypass his challengers by relying on an extensive network of loyal supporters. Because he was a *marja-e taghlid*, this network included thousands of clerics and seminarians (*talebs*) who propagated his religious and political views. Most were members of religious associations with deep ties to Qom and Iran's conservative bazaar community. These associations played a key role in keeping Khomeini's message alive and influential within Iran during his 14 years of exile and then in organizing the massive protests that eventually led to the Shah's overthrow.[4]

After he took power, Khomeini continued to rely on his personal network to consolidate and maintain his authority, as many of the individuals who were opposed to his vision came to dominate Iran's republican system of government.[5] Khomeini's network included clerics and seminarians, members of the powerful Revolutionary Council, the Revolutionary Courts, and the Islamist street militias and pressure groups that eventually became the Revolutionary Guards.

Khomeini recognized that much of his authority was due to his ability to keep one step above the factional jockeying characteristic of Iranian politics. As he developed his personal network, he made choices that reinforced his position of apparent neutrality, ensuring that all of the leading factions were represented. The Revolutionary Council, for

---

[4]   One of the most important and active of these organizations was the Coalition of Islamic Associations (*Heyat ha ye Motalefeh ye Islami*) (Moslem, 2002, p. 50), led by conservative and religious baazaris who were deeply dissatisfied with the Shah's domestic and foreign policies. Another part of the network, the SCC, created in 1977 (Moslem, 2002, p. 51), was one of the principal clerical associations responsible for organizing the pro-Khomeini protests. It has produced much of the Islamic Republic's top leadership, including Khamenei, Rafsanjani, former chief of the Guardian Council Ayatollah Mohammad Yazdi, and former parliamentary speaker Hodjatoleslam Ali Akbar Nateq-Nouri.

[5]   The *Motalefeh* and SCC continued to be key members. In addition, Khomeini drew much of his support from the Islamic Republic Party (IRP), which was created after the revolution to ensure that his vision of *velayat-e faghih* was enshrined within the Iranian constitution and new system of government. The IRP also produced much of the Islamic Republic's future leadership.

example, consisted of individuals who had been Khomeini's close advisors during his exile. Some of these—such figures as Abolhassan Bani-Sadr, Sadegh Qotbzadeh, and Ibrahim Yazdi—were members of revolutionary groups that did not totally share the Supreme Leader's views of an Islamist state. Others were ambitious mid-ranking clergymen, such as Khamenei, Rafsanjani, Ayatollah Mohammad Beheshti, and Ayatollah Morteza Motahari. Khomeini trusted them for their ideological loyalty to *velayat-e faghih* and their ability to implement his dictates within the new political system. They lacked the religious qualifications and recognition enjoyed by the older clergymen in Khomeini's personal network. But they had been largely responsible for directing the revolution's "infrastructure," including semiunderground Islamic associations, bazaari guilds, and militias dedicated to replacing the old regime with an Islamic system.

Over time, this expanded personal network became a fixture in the Islamic Republic's political system. It basically amounted to a shadow government that functioned alongside Iran's official republican state structure. At the center of this network was the "inner circle" formed by the elite Revolutionary Council, whose members held great influence over national decisionmaking. The events that transpired in the early revolutionary period demonstrate the extent of its sway. Initially, Khomeini supported the new government with Bani Sadr as its president. But because Bani Sadr and his supporters opposed a strict *velayat-e faghih*, Khomeini came to consider them as unacceptably "liberal" and a danger to his vision of Iran. By using the Revolutionary Council to bypass the formal government and run the country, he marginalized the first president, who eventually fled Iran.

The Revolutionary Courts, the Revolutionary Guards, and the omnipresent local *komitehs* (committees) who were all part of Khomeini's broader personal network played a similar role by usurping the judicial and law enforcement functions of the official Iranian government. The Revolutionary Guards effectively became the "shock troops" of Khomeini's *velayat-e faghih* by suppressing anti–*velayat-e faghih* forces and imposing his will on the opposition forces and republican institutions.

Khomeini's Personal Network Was the Main Driver of the 1989 Succession

When the question of a successor to Khomeini arose at the end of the 1980s, Khomeini's personal network was closely involved. Ultimately, the network—and particularly its inner circle—ensured that Khamenei was chosen to be Iran's Supreme Leader in 1989, as opposed to the candidate whom Khomeini had originally selected, Ayatollah Hossein Ali Montazeri.

Montazeri was a leading *marja* and had been one of Khomeini's most trusted aides within Iran on the eve of the revolution. After the Shah's overthrow, Khomeini tasked Montazeri with writing the constitution. Soon after, in 1985, Khomeini named him deputy Supreme Leader and his successor. Yet, although Montazeri was a revolutionary icon, a devoted follower of Khomeini's view of *velayat-e faghih*, and Khomeini's protégé, he was not an essential member of Khomeini's personal network, never finding a place among the influential inner circle.[6]

The powerful lower- and mid-ranking clergymen who formed that inner circle viewed Montazeri as a political novice, an incompetent bureaucrat, and an outsider.[7] Most importantly, they perceived Montazeri's rank as a leading *marja* as a threat to their influence. As top-ranking members of the Revolutionary Council, Rafsanjani and Khamenei, for example, wielded considerable political power but did not possess the necessary jurisprudential credentials to assume key government positions. Opposing Montazeri offered a potential pathway for them to rise to national prominence.

Montazeri did nothing to breach this gap, maintaining his distance from both the Revolutionary Council and the IRP.[8] At the end of Khomeini's life, he further dissociated himself from the inner circle

---

[6]   Shahrough Akhavi, "The Thought and Role of Ayatollah Hossein'ali Montazeri in the Politics of Post-1979 Iran," *Iranian Studies*, December 1, 2008.

[7]   As an example, they referred to the fact that although Montazeri was the chief of the Assembly of Experts, Khomeini had given the day-to-day responsibility of running the institution to Montazeri's deputy, Ayatollah Beheshti.

[8]   Akhavi, 2008.

when he began to publicly express his growing view that the Islamic Republic had deviated from the "true" course set by the revolutionaries. In effect, he became a critic of the political system that he himself had played a crucial role in creating. Although continuing to support Khomeini's *velayat-e faghih*, he called for a more open and participatory political system, criticizing the *nezam* and Khomeini himself for abusing human rights and mistreating Iranians.[9]

Montazeri's inability to navigate Khomeini's personal network was perhaps the most immediate reason for his eventual disentitlement as the Supreme Leader's heir. Rafsanjani and his supporters within Khomeini's inner circle were largely responsible for Montazeri's disqualification. The involvement of one of Montazeri's relatives in the Iran-Contra affair provided a convenient excuse for his opponents, especially Rafsanjani, to marginalize him further from power.[10] But Montazeri's criticism of Khomeini's involvement in the mass execution of leftist prisoners in 1988 proved his final undoing. This was the final straw for Khomeini and several close advisers in his personal network, including Rafsanjani and Khamenei. In a written response, Khomeini told Montazeri: "Since it has become clear to me that after me you are going to hand over this country [and] our dear Islamic revolution . . . to the liberals . . . you are no longer eligible to succeed me as the legitimate leader of the state."[11]

Rafsanjani benefited significantly from Montazeri's downfall, succeeding Khamenei as president for the next eight years and becoming one of the *nezam*'s richest and most powerful figures. And Khamenei quickly became the primary contender for the office of Supreme Leader. In many ways, he was Montazeri's opposite. He met Khomeini's and the inner circle's key qualifications for the position,[12] and he

---

[9]   Baqer Moin, *Khomeini: Life of the Ayatollah*, New York: Thomas Dunne Books, 1999, p. 280.

[10]   Shaul Bakhash, *The Reign of the Ayatollahs, Iran and the Islamic Factional Politics in Post-Khomeini Iran*, New York: Basic Books, 1986, p. 281.

[11]   Moin, 1999, p. 287.

[12]   A relatively capable administrator and bureaucratic infighter, Khamenei was one of Khomeini's coordinators within the revolutionary elite before Khomeini's return to Iran and

had formed a key alliance with figures in Khomeini's personal network on the Islamist Right, specifically Rafsanjani. Rafsanjani played a crucial role in Khamenei's appointment, in large part because he had Khomeini's ear as his confidant. As the Assembly of Experts met to select the next Supreme Leader, Rafsanjani informed it that Khomeini had revealed to him that Khamenei was his preference for the next Supreme Leader. Khomeini's son, Ahmad, who was close to Rafsanjani, also played an important part, publicly verifying Khomeini's choice of Khamenei: "While Khamenei was in North Korea, the Imam (Ayatollah Khomeini), saw him on television, his approach, his speeches and his discussions. It was very interesting for the Imam, who said that he [Khamenei] was truly worthy of the leadership."[13]

Since the Mid-1990s, Khamenei and His Personal Network Have Steadily Consolidated Authority and Are Now the Principal Decisionmakers in Iranian Politics

When he took office in 1989, Khamenei inherited Khomeini's personal network. He retained many of the same Friday prayer leaders employed by Khomeini, for example, preserving the loyalty of an influential group of clerics.[14] He has relied on many of the same conservative revolutionary associations that helped bring Khomeini to power, such as the *Motalefeh* and the SCC. He has drawn crucial support from the Association of Qom Seminary Teachers, which has produced some of the *nezam*'s most conservative figures, including Jannati and Ayatollah Mohammad Yazdi, the current and former chiefs of the Guardian Council. The Guardian Council has consistently acted in support of

---

played an important role in organizing the Islamist revolutionary forces that overthrew the Shah (Bakhash, 1986, p. 42). He held a number of important positions before assuming the Office of Supreme Leader, including Tehran's Friday prayer leader in 1979; Deputy Defense Minister and then supervisor of the Revolutionary Guards in 1980; and president from 1981 to 1989.

[13]   Moin, 1999, p. 310.

[14]   Buchta, 2000.

Khamenei's political objectives by vetting election candidates and suppressing reformist legislation.

But during his first years in office, Khamenei had little natural constituency of his own and had yet to put his personal imprimatur on the personal network that Khomeini (with his help) had cultivated and handed down to him. The clerical establishment that formed an important part of this network, for example, was irked by Khamenei's lack of religious scholarship and the fact that the constitution's original mandate that the Supreme Leader be a *marja-e taghlid*, or source of emulation, was dropped in order to allow Khamenei's appointment as Supreme Leader.[15]

Rafsanjani's presidency initially put a limit on Khamenei's authority, but over time Khamenei was able to assert himself. In addition, Khamenei and Rafsanjani managed to administer Iran without much of the friction that characterized Khamenei's relationship with Iran's next president, Mohammad Khatami. Khatami's election in 1997 surprised the *nezam*'s elite, including Khamenei. It signaled a rise of the Islamist Left to prominence, at least in the republican institutions and among those in the clerical establishment with democratic views of *velayat-e faghih*. This was viewed by Khamenei as a challenge to his role as Iran's supreme authority.

To counter this, Khamenei began to rely more heavily on those members of his personal network further to the right of the factional spectrum, trusting them to maintain the status quo and block the Islamist Left agenda that Khatami championed. Over time, he placed increasing numbers of these individuals in positions of power within the three branches of the government, the military and security forces (especially the Revolutionary Guards), and nongovernmental organiza-

---

[15]   He was certified as a *mujtahid* (jurist) after his selection as Supreme Leader by a relatively unknown clergyman, Muhammad Taqi Bahjat, who, according to Mehdi Khalaji, had not even taught Khamenei. Moreover, Ayatollah Muhammad Ali Araki was chosen as Khomeini's successor as *marja* by the ruling elite. An aging Ayatollah considered to be one of the highest-ranking *marjas* in Iran, Araki was viewed as being malleable and loyal by Khamenei and his clerical allies. Indeed, Araki's selection as *marja* after Khomeini's death in 1989 prevented the disbursement of Khomeini's religious authority among the various *marjas*, many of whom did not adhere to the absolute *velayat-e faghih*. Khamenei began to claim the status of a *marja* after Araki's death in 1994.

tions, such as the *bonyads*. In tandem, he slowly pushed out the reformists and even pragmatic conservatives who had been part of the network he had inherited from Khomeini. At the same time, he expanded his inner circle to include top principlist members of the Revolutionary Guards. His personal network began to take on a strong factional character.

The principlists within Khamenei's personal network played an instrumental role in getting Ahmadinejad elected as president in 2005. The Basij, for example, were widely accused of resorting to illegal activities, such as ballot stuffing and multiple voting using false birth certificates, to see Ahmadinejad emerge the winner.[16]

During Ahmadinejad's first term, Khamenei became steadily more dependent on extreme right figures and associations that accepted his authority based on the more absolutist concept of *velayat-e faghih*. These included hard-line principlist members of the clergy and Revolutionary Guards and such religious organizations as the Imam Khomeini Educational and Research Institute, headed by Ayatollah Mesbah-Yazdi, "dean" of the hard-line Islamist Right movement in Iran. This damaged Khamenei's credibility as a "balancer" or "arbitrator" of Iran's factional system of politics—a position Khomeini maintained relatively well.

As his role as an "arbitrator" has declined since 2005, Khamenei has increasingly relied on the Guards to buttress his dwindling religious and political authority. As a result, the Guards have become the arbitrator of political "correctness" in Iran and are used against *nezam* factions that have questioned the status quo. With the dispute over the 2009 election, the Revolutionary Guards, along with the Basij militia, have become a dominant part of Khamenei's personal network. In a speech given a few weeks before the June 12, 2009, election, Mojtaba Zolnour, one of Khamenei's representatives within the Guards, indicated his support for the incumbent Ahmadinejad.[17] In addition, Zol-

---

[16] Kasra Naji, *Ahmadinejad: The Secret History of Iran's Radical Leader*, Berkeley, Calif.: University of California Press, 2008, p. 77.

[17] "Janeshin Namayand e Vali e Faghih dar Sepah, ya Sokhanguy e Hezb e Siyasi Nezamian? [The Deputy Representative of the Supreme Leader in the Guards, or the Spokesper-

nour criticized several leading *nezam* figures, including Khatami, Rafsanjani, and even principlist Mohsen Rezai. Zolnour's comments may have represented the views of Khamenei. They suggested that neither Khameini nor his personal network considered any reformists or even principlists at that time to be legitimate presidential candidates.

The Guards' political bureau also played an important role in Ahmadinejad's reelection. Just days before the voting, the bureau's chief, General Yadollah Javani, announced that he viewed the reformist movement and its leading candidate, Mir Hussein Mousavi, as agents of a "velvet revolution" designed to overthrow the *nezam* and the *velayat-e faghih*. The Guards, he declared, would "snuff out" any attempts at a velvet revolution—i.e., a Mousavi victory.[18]

In the aftermath of the election, the Guards confirmed that they had acted to protect the revolution from the reformist "threat." According to the Guards' chief commander, General Ali Jaffari, "The Revolutionary Guards is tasked with defending the revolution and it has to play a determining role in protecting and eternalizing the revolution."[19] Javani stated that "Today, no one is impartial. There are two currents—those who defend and support the revolution and the establishment, and those who are trying to topple it."[20] The Basij led the *nezam*'s crackdown on the election protesters, showing themselves to be Khamenei's most loyal security forces.[21]

With these events, Khamenei empowered the Guards in a way that Khomeini may have never imagined—or even approved of. Principlists within the Revolutionary Guards emerged as the most powerful component of Khamenei's personal network. Khamenei's personal network in effect took the role of not only a state within a state but

---

son for the Military Political Party?" Agah Sazi, May 20, 2009.

[18] Thomas Erdbrink, "Rallies Close Out Iranian Campaign," *Washington Post*, June 11, 2009.

[19] Borzou Daraghi, "Iran's Revolutionary Guard Acknowledges Taking a Bigger Role in Nation's Security," Lebanon Wire, July 6, 2009.

[20] Daraghi, 2009.

[21] There were indications that the *Nirouhayeh Entezami* (Law Enforcement Forces) were reluctant to beat unarmed protesters.

also a "thought police" of sorts within Iran's institutions of power. It formed an insular and tightly knit decisionmaking circle dedicated to the preservation of the current political system and the more absolutist ideology of *velayat-e faghih*. This came not only at the expense of the reformists but also of traditional and pragmatic conservatives, such as Rafsanjani.

Five Scenarios for Succession of the Supreme Leader in the Near Term

The future of the institution of the Supreme Leader after Khamenei will depend on the three factors now exerting the strongest effect on the direction of the *nezam*: the balance of factional power, the prevailing view of *velayat-e faghih*, and the degree of influence of Khamenei's personal network. Analysts and policymakers can observe how each of these three factors develops individually, as well as configurations and reconfigurations of the three over time, as a means of determining the relative likelihood that any one of a number of scenarios will come to pass as succession approaches.

Each key factor can be viewed through the lens of a set of specific indicators that analysts can track and interpret over time. The indicators make it possible to assess how a given factor is unfolding, as well as the probable weight it will have in shaping succession. These indicators are the starting point for informed speculation about the likely character of the next Supreme Leader—or even whether the position will be abolished—and, by extension, the future direction of Iran.

Indicators That Suggest How Factional Competition Is Evolving

Analysts can keep track of the following indicators to get a sense of how the balance of power between the *nezam*'s main factions is unfolding and how factionalism could influence succession:

- *Dominance of a faction in government.* The hold a faction has on the presidency and the Majles, particularly during a succession process, may indicate the type of Supreme Leader that follows Khamenei.
- *Dominance of a faction in the Assembly of Experts and other key institutions.* The factional preferences of the 86 clerics in the assembly would contribute to determining the role that body would play in succession and its level of activism. Activism by other institutions, such as the Expediency Council, could affect the influence of factions in government and in the opposition.
- *Relationship between factions and the Supreme Leader.* The Supreme Leader's statements and actions may show support for or obstruction of factional interests. This may provide insight into what influence different factions wield. The relative success or failure of his preferences could also reveal factional power relationships.
- *Factional representation in the* nezam. This provides a sign of "how big the tent is" and, consequently, how much influence opposing factions might have in decisionmaking related to succession. The extent of government pressure on opposition factions, or, conversely, of tolerance for other factions, is an important determinant of how the Iranian constitution is interpreted and applied. The existence or absence of cross-factional alliances in the *nezam* may also help determine influence during succession.
- *Status and influence of groups outside the* nezam. The relative power and sway of such groups, such as the Green Movement, could actually help determine the future of the *nezam*, even though they do not currently form a part of it.
- *Status of republican institutions and civil society.* Expansion or contraction of civil society and weakening or strengthening of republican institutions are other indicators of how factional competition might shape succession.

Indicators That Point to the Prevailing View of *Velayat-e Faghih*

Any of the following indicators can illuminate which reading of *velayat-e faghih* is predominant within the *nezam* at a given time:

- *Statements by key clerics, or debates among them, related to divine authority, popular will, and the role of religion in the political system.* Such debates in various forums—Qom and Najaf, the Assembly of Experts, public speeches—can provide signs that any of the three forms of *velayat-e faghih* are increasing or declining in status and, consequently, portend their role in succession. The frequency and vociferousness of such statements and debates are important to consider.
- *The political and religious standing of individual clerics making such statements.* This may also provide clues about which schools of thought on *velayat-e faghih* are dominating or waning in influence.
- *Government responses to statements about* velayat-e faghih. The harshness or leniency with which the government reacts to statements or debates could signal dominance of a particular school of thought or, equally, fear that an opposing school of thought is gaining strength.
- *The government's use of* velayat-e faghih *in its own statements.* Increasing or decreasing use of *velayat-e faghih* in government policies and pronouncements may suggest how important a role the concept may play during succession.

Indicators That Signal How Khamenei's Personal Network Is Developing and the Power It Holds

Analysts can observe the following indicators to identify the level of influence that Khamenei, his inner circle, and his broader personal network may have in shaping the next succession:

- *Status of the Revolutionary Guards and the nature of its multiple roles in Iran.* The status of the Revolutionary Guards and the nature of its roles in politics, the economy, and society will significantly affect the part this organization plays in shaping succession. Observers may see its status in the frequency and types of statements made by the Guards' leadership, as well as in its actions pertaining to internal security, elections, and economic activity. Appearance of schisms and purges among the leadership would also serve as a key indicator of the Guards' direction.

- *Cohesiveness of statements and activities of the Supreme Leader's special representatives.* Whether or not institutional representatives, Friday prayer leaders, and other appointees speak with one voice will indicate the level of unity within Khamenei's personal network.

- *Status and activities of key individuals.* The types and frequency of the activities of individuals close to the Supreme Leader—either publicly or behind the scenes—may indicate whether a given individual is becoming more or less important in terms of succession.

- *Status of efforts at accountability.* The success or failure of initiatives to improve accountability in the system is a harbinger of the influence of Khamenei's personal network, which currently thrives on lack of accountability.

- *Status and activities of the Guardian Council.* Members of the Guardian Council, who are directly or indirectly appointed by the Supreme Leader, influence the course of legislation and elections and help determine the environment in which succession might take place.

- *Size and authorities of the Office of the Supreme Leader.* A large office with broad powers of administration would have considerable influence over the course of a succession.

- *Use of vigilante groups to intimidate opposition groups.* The appearance of multiple vigilante groups to intimidate, harass, and even murder opponents would suggest a personal network ready to work outside the system to protect itself and the Supreme Leader.

The Configuration of the Three Factors as of 2011

The lineup of the three factors in 2011 provides a baseline from which analysts can start tracking different possible trajectories toward the next succession. In terms of the factional balance of power, the principlists currently dominate the three branches of government—executive, legislative, and judicial. Principlist Khamenei loyalists and supporters of a more absolute *velayat-e faghih* are the backbone of the influential Guardian Council. The principlists also control the military and security forces, including the powerful Revolutionary Guards. In some ways, the Expediency Council, chaired by Rafsanjani, is still a bastion of the pragmatic conservatives, but at this time it does not appear to wield much authority. In theory, Rafsanjani's role as head of the Expediency Council and the Assembly of Experts should give him substantial leverage vis-à-vis Khamenei, Ahmadinejad, and other principlists. During the dispute over the 2009 election results, speculation was rife that he would use his position to pressure Khamenei to rein in Ahmadinejad. But, reportedly, he failed to have garnered enough backing within the assembly to either pressure or censure the Supreme Leader. Hard-line principlists, such as Mesbah-Yazdi and Ayatollah Ahmad Khatami (no relation to Mohammad Khatami), may have maintained sufficient power over the assembly during the post-election period to have thwarted their traditional-conservative and pragmatic-conservative counterparts. It appears that their influence is no less strong today.

The principlists, however, are currently deeply divided among themselves. For example, both the Majles and the judiciary are dominated by the Larijani brothers, who, although principlist in ideology, oppose Ahmadinejad. Ali Larijani, in particular, has competed fiercely with Ahmadinejad for political influence. When Ahmadinejad set out in 2010 to take control of the Azad University system, which is loosely affiliated with Rafsanjani and his supporters, the Majles actually attempted to block his plan. In response, pro-Ahmadinejad vigilantes protested in front of parliament, branding some members as "traitors."[1]

---

[1]   "Iran University Reform Sparks Row in Ahmadinejad Camp," BBC News, June 23, 2010.

Larijani and other anti-Ahmadinejad principlist figures, such as Expediency Council Secretary Mohsen Rezai and Tehran Mayor Mohammad Bagher Ghalibaf, would like to limit the current president's power and perhaps ensure an outcome more favorable to them in the 2013 presidential election.

Yet in spite of these internal fissures within the hard-line right, the Supreme Leader continues to support Ahmadinejad and his followers. This support has decisively shaped the factional balance of power today: As a result, the Islamist Left and the Green Movement have been effectively marginalized, while prominent and often loyal pragmatic-conservative, and even principlist, leaders, such as Rafsanjani and Larijani, have lost a great deal of standing. Indeed, what power Rafsanjani will hold within the system in the next few years is now unclear.

Khamenei's resolute backing of Ahmadinejad during the 2009 election, echoed by prominent principlist clerics, such as Mesbah-Yazdi, is likely to have a decisive influence on a near-term succession: The faction that currently controls the *nezam*'s institutions, and that faction's viewpoint on *velayat-e faghih*, will have a key role in shaping what comes after Khamenei. The presidency, in particular, is a valued prize for the principlists and supporters of the absolute *velayat-e faghih*. Ahmadinejad is now positioned to influence the succession, should it happen in the next several years. This authority is formalized in the Iranian constitution, which stipulates that

> in the event of the death, or resignation or dismissal of the Leader, the experts shall take steps within the shortest possible time for the appointment of the new Leader. Until the appointment of the new Leader, a council consisting of the President, head of the judiciary, and a religious man from the Guardian Council, upon the decision of the Nation's Expediency Council, shall temporarily take over all the duties of the Leader.[2]

In this light, a Mousavi victory in the 2009 presidential election would have in many ways realized the principlists' worst nightmare, because it would have paired a reformist presidency with the

---

[2]   See Algar, 1980a.

pragmatic conservative Rafsanjani's control of the Assembly of Experts and the Expediency Council. Indeed, Rafsanjani's decision to side with Mousavi and the reformists in the election's aftermath may have been motivated by political expediency (after all, Rafsanjani had been the bane of the reformist movement during Khatami's presidency). But in terms of the factional balance of power, it has nevertheless shown that at this point in time, the pragmatic conservatives and the reformists share common concerns about the Islamic Republic's fate and long-term interests.

With regard to *velayat-e faghih*, the absolute interpretation is currently predominant within the Islamic Republic. This is in line with the consolidation of power by the principlists, who favor this interpretation. Although the concept was at times debated vigorously during the 1990s, the rise of the Revolutionary Guards, the marginalization of the reformists and pragmatic conservatives, and the weakening of Iran's competing power centers over the last decade have now created fertile ground for this more narrow and authoritarian interpretation of *velayat-e faghih*.

As one of the chief spokesmen for the absolute *velayat-e faghih*, Mesbah-Yazdi vocally maintains that the Supreme Leader is the ultimate and undisputed source of authority within Iran. Indeed, he has asserted this position consistently since the 2009 election. Ahmadinejad has echoed his view, declaring in July 2010 that the only party in Iran is that of the *velayat*, meaning Khamenei.[3] The Supreme Leader himself issued a *fatwa* that same month stressing his role as the spiritual heir to the Prophet Muhammad and the Twelve Imams: This *fatwa* explicitly states that the people must obey him in the absence of the Hidden Imam.[4]

The deaths or marginalization in 2009 of leading proponents of the two other interpretations of *velayat-e faghih* have only served to entrench the absolutist view more firmly. Ayatollah Montazeri, who

---

[3]   Alistair Lyon, "Analysis—Iran's President Angers Conservatives, Reformists," Reuters, July 19, 2010.

[4]   Nazanin Kamdar, "Khamenei's Fatwa About Himself: You Must Obey Me," Rooz Online, July 23, 2010.

passed away in December 2009, was perhaps the most emulated and respected advocate of democratic *velayat-e faghih*. But his "successor," Ayatollah Yousef Sanei, now faces intense pressure from supporters of the absolute interpretation to stop advocating the democratic interpretation. The Association of Qom Seminary Teachers, which staunchly supports the absolute perspective, has attempted to undermine Sanei's role as a source of emulation.[5] Other traditionalist- and reformist-leaning members of the clergy are facing similar pressure over their views on *velayat-e faghih*, while a number of Friday prayer leaders critical of the status quo reading of the concept plan to go into "retirement" in the near future.[6]

Outside the religious sphere, influential political figures with close ties to either the traditionalist or reformist clergy who support a more democratic view of *velayat-e faghih* have also lost much influence since the 2009 election. Rafsanjani is perhaps the leading example—one of the few figures within the Islamic Republic who might have had the power and standing to effectively challenge absolute *velayat-e faghih*. Individuals in the democratic camp have spoken of a Leadership Council and a greater role for senior clergymen, either of which would threaten Khamenei's absolute vision of *velayat-e faghih*. Rafsanjani and reformist leaders have repeatedly highlighted the "republican" and popular aspects of the Islamic Republic as an essential part of its Islamist character. For example, in his much-anticipated post-election Friday prayer speech on June 17, 2009, Rafsanjani declared that

> according to the constitution, everything in the country is determined by [the] people's vote. People elect the members of the Assembly of Experts and then they elect [the] leader, that is, [the] leader is [indirectly] elected by [the] people's vote. Presidents, MPs, members of the councils are elected by direct votes of [the] people. Other officials are also appointed [indirectly] through [the] people's vote. Everything depends on people. This is the reli-

---

[5]   "Iranian Dissident Cleric Condemns Government Intimidations," Radio Zamaneh, May 9, 2010.

[6]   Kayvan Bozorgmehr, "Iran: The Great Purge of Friday Prayer Leaders," Rooz Online, July 28, 2010.

gious system. The title of Islamic Republic is not used as a formality. It includes both the republican and Islamic nature.[7]

Rafsanjani's take on *velayat-e faghih* and the Islamic Republic is markedly different from that of the hard-liners who have supported Khamenei and Ahmadinejad. In response to Rafsanjani's speech, Ayatollah Mohammad Yazdi replied that the "[p]eople's support doesn't bring legitimacy, but popularity."[8] According to Yazdi, the Islamic Republic's legitimacy is not based on popular will or the constitution but rather on the authority conferred by God to the *vali-e faghih*. The quietist or democratic visions of *velayat-e faghih* have no room in the worldview of such men as Yazdi, which is currently preeminent in Iran.

Yet the democratic view today remains relevant. Even though at times the Islamist Left has been critical of *velayat-e faghih*, it has never advocated the quietist interpretation and consequently still operates within the "red line" that the concept forms in today's Islamic Republic. For this reason, Khamenei and the Islamist Right have not been able to fully extinguish the reformists' participation in the political system. Accordingly, the notion of a democratic *velayat-e faghih* today possesses a certain sense of legitimacy, though it remains on the margins of Iranian politics. Indeed, it may resonate more strongly with average Iranians, especially groups who have been excluded from the political system, including the young, women, secularists, and ethnic and religious minorities. In this sense, democratic *velayat-e faghih* has the potential eventually to be viewed not only as a religious-ideological doctrine but also as a more practical answer to Iran's evolving socioeconomic needs—especially as the *nezam* struggles with popular pressures and expectations. With backing from some of Iran's top religious authorities, including (until his death) Montazeri and Grand Ayatollah Yousef Sanei, the democratic *velayat-e faghih* may have the necessary

---

[7] "Iran: Full Text of Rafsanjani's Lengthy Speech," *Los Angeles Times* web log, June 17, 2009.

[8] Ali Akbar Dareini, "Hard-Liners Accuse Top Iranian Cleric of Defiance," Associated Press, July 19, 2009.

jurisprudential support to be relevant if the next succession happens in the next two to three years.

Finally, in terms of Khamenei's personal network, it is at present fully merged with his factional affiliation. Khamenei's network is now composed primarily of pro-Ahmadinejad principlists who share a common vision and objective: to preserve his standing as Iran's absolute political and religious authority. This fusion of the two may be largely what has been driving his support for Ahmadinejad over the past year and a half. The disproportionate weight of the Revolutionary Guards, which is at present both the most powerful element in Khamenei's personal network *and* dominated by pro-Ahmadinejad principlists, may have done much to spur the Supreme Leader to take such a high-profile stance in favor of Ahmadinejad during the 2009 election. Indeed, the Guards' commander in chief, Ali Jaffari, appears to have played a pivotal role in the election's final outcome.

Khamenei may also have taken both succession and his age into consideration when he explicitly endorsed Ahmadinejad as the victor in 2009. For Khamenei, such reformists as Khatami, Karroubi, and Mousavi have come to represent a real threat to his legacy and vision for the Islamic Republic. Karroubi, for instance, spoke of changing the constitution during his 2009 presidential campaign. He could have fundamentally altered the *nezam*'s political status quo if he became president.[9]

Rather than serving as a break with the past, the 2009 election solidified a trend that has been developing at least since Khatami's administration in the 1990s: Although *velayat-e faghih* continues officially to be the ideological foundation of Iran's system of Islamist rule, politics in the Islamic Republic is now based much more on informal personal connections than on religious-ideological tenets. Khamenei and his personal network, including elements of the Revolutionary Guards, are now governing the Iranian state much like governments in many other countries in the developing world—that is, without resorting to the rule of law and foundational ideologies to gain legitimacy. Indeed, Khamenei has shown that he is willing to contravene the

---

[9]   "Karrubi Talks of Constitutional Reform," Rooz Online, April 20, 2009.

nezam's core structures and principles in order to cement his personal rule and protect the gains of his network of supporters.

Still, the current dominance of Khamenei, Ahmadinejad, and the principlists is not assured in the future. The clergy in Qom and other important religious institutions and associations are dissatisfied with the status quo and Iran's increasingly militarized and authoritarian political system. The Assembly of Experts, though conservative in nature, is composed of clerics who may view the absolute version of *velayat-e faghih* with consternation, as it subjugates their own religious and political influence to Khamenei and the Revolutionary Guards. Although marginalized, the Green Movement today remains a viable social and political opposition force. Mousavi, Karroubi, and Khatami retain at least some popularity among the middle class, the intelligentsia, students, and women's rights activists. Finally, Iran's civil society remains relatively strong and intermittently resists government suppression.

Five Possible Scenarios for Succession of the Current Supreme Leader

Our analysis of the key factors and various leadership concepts that have been discussed at times in Iran suggest five scenarios for succession over the next two to three years. These five cover as much of the "scenario space" as is practicable:

- *status quo*, in which Khamenei is followed by a leader like himself, possibly someone he handpicks
- *absolutist*, in which Khamenei's successor is a dictatorial leader with strong religious and political credentials supported by a cult of personality
- *democratic,* in which the next Supreme Leader is a reformist who is more accountable than the current Supreme Leader to Iran's republican institutions and the electorate
- *Leadership Council*, in which an executive leadership group replaces a single leader

- *abolition*, which sees the demise of the Supreme Leader position in favor of republicanism.

The first four scenarios represent leadership options that the Islamic Republic could portray as occurring within the framework of the Islamic Revolution and *velayat-e faghih*. In other words, a new political system could make the case that any one of these four options is founded upon the legacy of Ayatollah Ruhollah Khomeini and the "true" aims of the Islamic Revolution (according to the *nezam*'s interpretation).[10] The fifth scenario, abolition, represents the end of the Islamic Republic as it exists today.

All five of these scenarios are plausible, although they are not equally likely to come about. The odds that any one in particular would come to pass would depend on how the three key factors are configured in the months preceding Khamenei's departure from the scene. But these scenarios are by no means predictive: Post-Khamenei Iran will very likely not be an exact replica of any one of the five; more likely, it will look like some adaptation of one of them.

Each of the three key factors may change in different possible ways over the next several years, affecting the other two and bringing about new configurations. Different developments in the factors describe various trajectories—in effect, storylines—that could lead to the five scenarios (see Figure 5.1). As new configurations of the factors emerge, they provide clues about the increasing or decreasing likelihood that a particular scenario—or something like it—will come to fruition. By keeping an eye on the indicators associated with the factors, analysts can keep pace with developments and make informed estimates of what kind of Supreme Leader might emerge from a near-term succession process.

Each of the five possible end states we describe would differ along a number of lines:

---

[10] Just as the most pro-Mousavi reformists and the most pro-Ahmadinejad principlists both claim that their platforms derive from Khomeini—they seek to operate within the broad framework of the Islamic Republic.

Figure 5.1
Possible Trajectories for Succession of the Supreme Leader in the Next Two to Three Years (within the current presidential term)

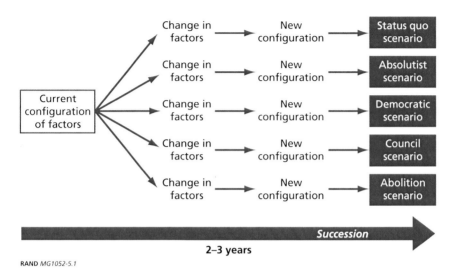

- the nature and source of the Supreme Leader's legitimacy and executive power
- his role in decisionmaking and the level of control he exerts over the affairs of state and Iranian society
- his ideology, factional tendencies, and worldview
- the requirements for change to the 1989 constitution
- the personal background of candidates appropriate for the type of leadership involved
- the potential consequences of the leadership type for Iran's internal political system.

Status Quo: The Supreme Leader Remains Powerful But Not Omnipotent

The status quo scenario involves a Supreme Leader whose nature, role, and authorities would resemble those of the Supreme Leader today. A status quo end state after Khamenei's passing would be characterized by continued consolidation of Khamenei's factional preferences, empowerment of elements of his personal network (including the

Revolutionary Guards), and continued emphasis on a more absolutist interpretation of *velayat-e faghih*. Should this scenario come to pass, it would suggest that Khamenei and his supporters had maximum influence on the configuration of factors.

In terms of the balance of factional power, the stage is set for a narrowing of factional participation in the shaping of succession. The continued dominance of hard-line principlists under Ahmadinejad in the *nezam*'s republican institutions, especially the presidency, is one clear indicator of this. In a trajectory toward a status quo outcome, for example, principlists, with Khamenei's blessing, would likely seek to eliminate opposition groups from the system. Government security organs might suppress opposition factions—including reformists and pragmatic conservatives—through arrests, shuttering of media outlets, and prosecution under sedition laws. The government would openly suspend opposition groups, and leading Green Movement figures, such as Mousavi and Karroubi, would be arrested, thus "beheading" the opposition. Civil society would also likely be increasingly restricted. Opposition factions would continue to be active and to hold demonstrations periodically in spite of the restrictions, but they would be largely excluded from the political system.

The Supreme Leader's public comments related to factional conflict could indicate the dominance of one faction over another—for example, if Khamenei were to express support for pro-Ahmadinejad principlists in the event of government criticism by more moderate or technocratic principlists. In this trajectory, Islamist Left groups, such as the Islamic Iran Participation Front, and even pragmatic conservative Islamist Right groups, such as the Rafsanjani-affiliated *Kargozaran-e Sazandegi*, would increasingly bear the brunt of the *nezam*'s crackdown on opposition groups. Other Islamist Right figures, such as former chief commander of the Revolutionary Guards and presidential candidate Mohsen Rezai, would also continue to be marginalized from the political system. Even Ali Larijani, the principlist speaker of the Majles and a trusted Khamenei associate, would continue to see his authority challenged by Khamenei's support for Ahmadinejad.

In sum, to arrive at the status quo scenario, the balance of factional power would unfold in such a way that the Islamist Right principlist faction that currently dominates the Iranian government would attempt to exclude such figures as Rafsanjani from decisionmaking during the next succession. After all, the faction ruling Iran today considers Rafsanjani, once the paragon of the Islamist Revolution, to have become an "outsider," just as Montazeri was labeled in 1988, several months before Khomeini's passing.

With regard to the second factor, *velayat-e faghih*, in the trajectory toward the status quo, the absolutist interpretation would serve as a means for Khamenei to enforce his claim to not only his own religious legitimacy but also that of a future Supreme Leader. Because it is the interpretation most closely associated with Ayatollah Khomeini, the absolutist *velayat-e faghih* holds the most resonance among Iran's more–ideologically motivated revolutionary establishment. In this trajectory, one might see Khamenei and the principlists on the Islamist Right continuing to drive the ideological discourse on *velayat-e faghih* via the latter's domination of key institutions, including the Assembly of Experts, the Guardian Council, and various Qom seminaries. The principlists would paint the traditional and democratic discourse on *velayat-e faghih* as counterrevolutionary and would stifle public debate on alternative forms of the concept that run counter to the absolutist version.

To strengthen its interpretation of *velayat-e faghih*, for example, the government could bring pressure to bear on clerics in Qom who supported democratic or quietist views of *velayat-e faghih*—possibly to include widened use of the Special Court for the Clergy as a means of silencing opponents of Khamenei and the absolutist interpretation. Key clerical supporters of Khamenei and the Islamist Right (such as Jannati and Mesbah-Yazdi) might issue statements and speeches referring to diminution of public will in the rule of the jurisprudent and emphasizing the special nature of the Islamic Republic as a religious system. Another indicator would be the house arrest of clerical and lay opponents who questioned Khamenei's religious legitimacy on charges of counterrevolutionary activities.

Khamenei's personal network would play a very strong role in setting the stage for a status quo succession. One would see key institutions or entities closely tied to Khamenei reinforcing the Supreme

Leader's power base and weakening potential challengers. For example, the Revolutionary Guards leadership would continue to express unfettered support for the Supreme Leader while at the same time retaining or increasing its involvement in political, economic, security, and military matters. The Supreme Leader's representatives within the Guards might be quoted as declaring that they would forcibly prevent a "velvet revolution," as they did before the 2009 election. The Guardian Council would approve mainly Islamist Right candidates for elections. Finally, key individuals within Khamenei's inner circle would make an increasing number of public appearances and would be appointed to critical positions—such as special representative to the Supreme National Security Council—all portending a consolidation of Khamenei's power.

As a result of this sequence of developments, the factors would configure within the next two to three years in a way that allowed key individuals from a substantially narrowed spectrum of factions and Khamenei's personal network to limit the circle of those shaping the next succession. Indeed, factional competition and Khamenei's personal network would have a much more direct influence on succession than the prevailing view of *velayat-e faghih*. Khamenei himself would have the most important say. A small circle of hard-line principlists and Guards leaders might work, for example, to push Khamenei's preferred candidate for Supreme Leader through the succession process. At the same time, security organs might harass alternative candidates and their supporters as accusations about supposed illegal activities were brought to light. Members of "moderate" institutions might find their positions in jeopardy and act accordingly; for instance, fearing for their own positions of privilege, members of the traditional conservative-leaning Assembly of Experts could rubber-stamp the choice of Supreme Leader while Chairman Rafsanjani was absent from the proceedings.

Still, religious credentials would remain a primary requirement for the position. Khamenei and his personal network might have to choose a candidate who possessed some of the religious qualifications specified by the Iranian constitution, but this candidate would meet their factional and ideological criteria.

The outcome of all of this would be the status quo: a next Supreme Leader who resembles Khamenei in terms of qualifications, ideology, and role in decisionmaking. In this scenario, the Supreme Leader would remain the ultimate political authority, whose legitimacy is based on an interpretation of Khomeini's *velayat-e faghih*. But while his role would be considered divinely ordained, elected institutions would have some power. He would give some, however minor, consideration to popular opinion in his decisions and guidance, and republicanism would remain an important part of the bifurcated political system.

Officially, this status quo next Supreme Leader would be the chief jurisprudential authority of Iran and could even have greater religious standing than Khamenei. But other clerics and religious power centers could challenge that authority—occasionally in overt ways. The Supreme Leader would rely on both his own personal network and the one he inherited from Khamenei (which would include the upper echelon of the Revolutionary Guards) to ensure that such challenges to his position or legitimacy would be quelled rapidly and in ways that would ensure that the system remained stable.

In terms of policymaking, the next Supreme Leader in a status quo scenario would guide the overall policy of the Islamic Republic. He would be the commander in chief of the armed forces and would appoint all top commanders. He would have direct control over national security matters and most government activities through his personal network. Although the Supreme National Security Council would debate key national security issues, the Supreme Leader would make the important decisions. On domestic policy, the elected institutions would ostensibly set the country's economic and budgetary direction and manage the day-to-day business of government. But the Supreme Leader would intervene on domestic and social issues when they contradicted his guidance or when challenges arose that he believed put the stability of the system at risk.

The ideology of the next Supreme Leader in the status quo scenario would be based—as is Khamenei's currently—on the centrality of the Islamic Revolution as a defining concept of governance and would tend toward an anti-Western, isolationist view of the world. Revolutionary rhetoric about resistance to "bullying powers" (including the United States) would continue, even should relations with the West slowly start to thaw. Socially, the Supreme Leader would be conservative and would continue to stress "traditional" Islamic values and adherence to state-defined norms of political and social behavior. He would retain influence over traditional conservatives in the clerical establishment but would also rely on them to buttress his influence and legitimacy.

Inherently, the status quo scenario would involve minimal constitutional change. Any changes would reflect efforts to redefine certain qualities of the new Supreme Leader either that the *nezam* sought to emphasize (much as the 1989 constitution downgraded the Supreme Leader's religious standing to pave the way for Khamenei to assume the position) and/or that would codify emerging trends—for example, providing the Revolutionary Guards with enhanced powers and involvement in domestic political and security issues. But, by and large, the constitution would be similar to the version revised in 1989.

A likely candidate for Supreme Leader in this scenario is a conservative cleric of mid- to high-ranking religious status. He would hail either from the revolutionary "men's club" that has held positions of power in Iran since 1979 or from Khamenei's elite inner circle. He could even be handpicked by Khamenei. Examples of this type of candidate would be such figures as Ayatollah Ahmad Khatami or Ayatollah Jannati. In light of the symbiotic relationship between the Revolutionary Guards and Khamenei, as well as the Guards' increasing dominance over national security decisionmaking and internal security activities, the Guards' leadership may play the role of "kingmaker" and "approve" of the new Supreme Leader.

The internal political dynamics under the status quo scenario would continue to be marked by factionalism and competition among power centers. However, the Islamist Left would be largely purged from *nezam* policymaking, which would remain relatively static and dysfunctional. The Revolutionary Guards would play an even larger role in decisionmaking, internal security, and repression of dissent than they do today. At the same time, the new Supreme Leader could be relatively weak politically in the initial phases of his rule, just as Khamenei was after his appointment in 1989. It could take the new

Supreme Leader months—or even years—to consolidate his authority and incorporate Khamenei's networks and other power centers into his own sphere of influence. In the interim, he would be susceptible to manipulation, particularly by the Guards. He would have to account for the opinions and positions of the prevailing factions and power centers in his policy guidance and decisionmaking. Some instability in the system would be expected, but this could wane as the Supreme Leader and the other power centers established a new balance, with the former retaining the final word on core interests of the state.

Absolutist: The Supreme Leader, a Dictator, Discards Elected Institutions

The absolutist scenario would involve a Supreme Leader who combined the religious legitimacy of Ayatollah Khomeini with authoritarian one-man rule. He would be dictatorial, would dismantle the bifurcated institutional political system, and would lead in a much more authoritarian manner than his two predecessors. Absolutist views of *velayat-e faghih* and governance advocated by Ayatollah Mesbah-Yazdi and other radical elements of the Islamist Right would form the basis of this scenario.

As in the status quo scenario, the trajectory toward an absolutist scenario would be marked by a narrowing of factional representation in the *nezam* and, ultimately, in decisionmaking about succession. But here the narrowing would be more pronounced. In terms of the balance of factional power, all factions except for the hard-line Islamist Right would be pushed out of the system, including ostensibly principlist (particularly technocratic) groups. One would see the Iranian government taking more draconian measures to stifle dissent and consolidate power in the hands of a narrow decisionmaking group that would include Khamenei. Some elements of the constitution might be "temporarily suspended"—ostensibly for national security reasons. Other elements could be interpreted very narrowly, with freedoms that were previously permitted now being judged as "detrimental to the fundamental principles of Islam."

Government security organs in this trajectory would suppress opposition factions through arrests, shuttering of media outlets, and prosecution under sedition laws. Demonstrations by opposition factions would likely be banned; demonstrations or opposition gatherings that did occur would be quashed immediately, sometimes violently. Individuals in positions of institutional power from more moderate factions would be pushed out. For example, key figures associated with the Islamic Revolution's "men's club"—such as Rafsanjani—might be arrested and jailed for conspiring against the state. A new chairman of the Assembly of Experts might be elected from the far Islamist Right (a likely candidate would be Mesbah-Yazdi), putting the assembly squarely in the hands of hard-line principlists. These moves would be accompanied by a programmatic weakening of republican institutions to ensure that the hard-liners maintained control. Indicators might include efforts by the Guardian Council to disqualify all but the most right wing of candidates for election to the Majles, or even decisions by the government to postpone or cancel Majles and/or presidential elections on national security grounds.

With regard to *velayat-e faghih*, it would be a more prominent factor in the absolutist scenario than in the status quo scenario, serving as the foundational justification for the rise of a clerical dictator who would shroud himself in religious and revolutionary symbolism. Absolutist views of *velayat-e faghih* would become more dominant in public interactions and would be increasingly emphasized as the "true legacy" of Khomeini and the Revolution, while other views would be actively suppressed. For instance, heavy use of the absolutist interpretation of *velayat-e faghih*—that the Supreme Jurisprudent is directly "appointed" by God—would testify to the growing weight of the concept. Likewise, the government could bring pressure to bear on clerics in Qom who supported democratic or quietist views of *velayat-e faghih*. This might include widened use of the Special Court for the Clergy as a means of silencing opponents of Khamenei and the absolutist interpretation. Key clerical supporters of Khamenei and the Islamist Right (including Jannati and Mesbah-Yazdi) might make statements and speeches referring to diminution of public will in the rule of the jurisprudent and emphasizing the special nature of the Islamic Republic as not actually a republic but an Islamic state. Finally, clerical and lay opponents who questioned Khamenei's religious legitimacy might be placed under house arrest for counterrevolutionary activities, while some supporters of democratic and quietist views of *velayat-e faghih* might be exiled.

In the midst of all of this, a "rising star" could appear who would gain favor with Khamenei. He would be either someone whom Khamenei would actively select (in secret) as a successor or who would appear to be gaining such power and influence that Khamenei would attempt to co-opt him. This "rising star" would likely be a charismatic, learned, hard-line cleric with a strong personal network, some popularity among groups in the *nezam*, and supporters in the larger population. If the personal network of this future absolutist Supreme Leader overlapped with Khamenei's, it could set the stage for a rapid succession when Khamenei passed from the scene.

This cleric could already be in a position of power before that time came, with a number of signs pointing to his succession. One such route might stem from perceptions of Ahmadinejad's incompetence and rising societal and economic pressures. Together, these developments would prompt Khamenei to "replace" Ahmadinejad with the "rising star." This new president might then subsequently reinforce his popularity by championing economic and social initiatives that many constituents and elements of the government perceived as successful.

Additional efforts by both the Supreme Leader and this new president might be designed to consolidate each's personal power, along with that of their personal networks. Indicators could be actions similar to Khomeini's during the initial months and years of the Islamic Revolution. For example, this new hard-line cleric president could use personal security forces (vigilante groups, some of which would be linked to the Revolutionary Guards) to intimidate and silence opponents. He might create new decisionmaking entities outside the existing institutional framework, ostensibly with Khamenei's blessing. A "revolutionary council," headed by the cleric, might be formed, made up of individuals close to both Khamenei and the president from the Haqqani complex, the Ministry of Intelligence, the Revolutionary Guards, and hard-liners in the Assembly of Experts. At some point— possibly as succession was taking place—this council could take over internal security functions.

Of the three factors, the Supreme Leader's personal network and *velayat-e faghih* are the two that would predominantly shape succession in the absolutist scenario. The combination of a hard-line cleric bolstered by Khamenei's strong personal network (overlapping with the cleric's own) and a broad consensus on absolutist *velayat-e faghih* (at least among those who remained part of the political system) could propel the cleric into the position of Supreme Leader. If this cleric were president first, he might use the revolutionary council, which maintains its allegiance to him, to take over mechanisms of the state. The Assembly of Experts, with some members under duress, could unanimously declare him Supreme Leader.

Should this happen, *velayat-e faghih* would remain the basis of leadership and government in the Islamic Republic, but the new Supreme Leader would adopt the hard-line Islamist Right's interpretation of a truly absolute jurisprudent. On the basis of this strict interpretation of the *motlagh* (absolute) view, the Supreme Leader would be divinely ordained and accountable only to God. Popular opinion and political participation would therefore be unimportant and, in fact, unnecessary.

The absolutist Supreme Leader would be politically all-powerful. He would have direct control over national security, as well as foreign and domestic policy. He would also retain absolute authority over religious matters. He would retain a cadre of advisors on all matters of state and oversee a bureaucracy that would carry out his edicts and conduct the day-to-day management of the government.

This new Supreme Leader would be strongly conservative—even extreme—in his views of religion and the outside world. He would frame his decisions in revolutionary and religious terms, although nationalism could be an undercurrent. He would be anti-Western, anti-Israeli, anti-Sunni, and reactionary. Internally, he would see Western cultural influence and secularism as a grave threat to the Islamic Revolution and would consider revolutionary "principles" and freedom from foreign influence as essential to the *nezam*'s survival.

The constitution would need to be changed significantly in this absolutist scenario. The Islamic Revolution would remain the point of reference, but framers of this revised constitution would expunge references to a president, a parliament, elections, and the people's rights. Iran would still have an Islamic government, but references to a "republic" would be struck. Moreover, the constitution would alter the theocratic structure of the *nezam* by doing away with the Guardian and Expediency Councils (as there would no longer be a Majles to draft legislation or elections to oversee) and changing the nature of the Assembly of Experts. Since the clergy could no longer supervise or oversee the activities of a divinely ordained Supreme Leader, the constitution would perhaps reshape the assembly into a council to "advise" the Supreme Leader. It would be composed of clerics whom he appointed. The absolutist Supreme Leader would also appoint government ministers directly. Finally, a constitutional process for succession would perhaps be outlined in which the Supreme Leader would formally, and perhaps secretly, select a successor.

The likely candidate for the absolutist Supreme Leader would be a dynamic, ultra-conservative cleric—possibly of low to high rank and claiming to be a *marja*—who had built a cult of personality around himself. He would have his own networks and backing from right-wing clerical groups and elements of the security apparatus (particularly the Revolutionary Guards, the Basij, and unofficial "pressure" groups). He might be a member of the second generation of revolutionaries and would not necessarily be a member of the so-called "men's club" that had ruled the Islamic Republic since its inception. Ayatollah Mesbah-Yazdi or a protégé would be ideal candidates for this type of Supreme Leader.

With regard to internal political dynamics, the absolutist Supreme Leader would crush any challenges to his political and religious authority—at times ruthlessly—through a bolstered security apparatus and a system of religious courts that would quickly prosecute dissenters. Thus, dissent from Qom and opposition political factions would be brutally suppressed. Factionalism would be less prevalent than today and certainly would have little bearing on how decisions were made. Policymaking would be coherent and top-down but also ideological and assertive, driven by the Supreme Leader's ideology. The *nezam* would become an exclusionary political system, and repression would increase. In terms of foreign relations, Iran would focus on exporting the revolution and on real or imagined subversion from abroad. Under these circumstances, confrontation with the West would become even more likely than it is today.

In sum, the absolutist scenario would come about through a combination of a very exclusive, pro-absolute *velayat-e faghih* faction dominating the *nezam* and a confluence of interests between two very powerful personal networks—one Khamenei's and the other that of a charismatic, Khomeini-like figure who shrouded himself in a "cult of personality."

Democratic: An Iranian-Stylized Islamic Democracy

Far from introducing democracy in the Western sense, the democratic scenario would entail a "rebalancing" of the bifurcation between the elected and the unelected, or between the republican and the theocratic components of the Iranian political system. A hallmark of this scenario would be greater accountability to elected institutions and the people from the Supreme Leader and the theocratic component of the *nezam* that he heads.

The trajectory toward the democratic scenario would begin with a broadening of factional representation in the *nezam*. This would set the stage for the Islamist Left to influence the selection of the next Supreme Leader. Here, continuing efforts by opposition factions and groups to apply pressure for reform would be met increasingly with weaker government responses, followed by an evolution in factional relationships. Demonstrations could again become widespread, gaining support from key individuals and power centers in government, society, and the clerical establishment. Factional groups would likely form new alliances, with technocratic principlists joining pragmatic conservatives on certain policy issues.

Compromise and a new understanding between the government and the Islamist Left—possibly in the name of sustaining the Islamic Republic—would change the dynamic of factional politics. Reformist groups that had been suspended in the aftermath of the 2009 presidential election might be officially reinstated. Hard-line principlists could lose seats during elections to Majles and city councils to reformist, pragmatic conservative, and breakaway technocratic principlist candidates. Some of the latter might be moderate-leaning Guards alumni. Evolving institutional priorities and relationships would reflect these changes in political dynamics. For example, the Expediency Council under Rafsanjani might become more active in settling legislative disputes between the Majles and the Guardian Council and might often side with the former. The Expediency Council and the Majles could also conduct public reviews of government policies.

Similarly, the Assembly of Experts would likely take a more activist role, spearheaded by the vision that its chief, Rafsanjani, had laid out in the late 2000s. After he was selected as the assembly's head in July 2007, Rafsanjani reaffirmed the assembly's role in oversight and succession by stating that it "gives us the best mechanism for choosing the leader. . . . At the present moment it should not shirk from the responsibility to investigate the [characteristics] of those qualified to serve as the Supreme Leader, the same way it did in a matter of hours back in 1989."[11] At the time, Rafsanjani's statement gave notice to his political opponents—principlists centered around Ayatollah Mesbah-Yazdi and President Ahmadinejad—that the assembly, and more importantly Rafsanjani, would play a pivotal part in shaping the *nezam*'s future direction. Rafsanjani, as the dean of the "moderate" Islamic Right and the pragmatic conservatives, also indicated that the assembly might become involved in daily issues of government, such as the economy. This was somewhat unusual, given the assembly's rather strict and circumscribed constitutional mandate of selecting the Supreme Leader. Rafsanjani's allusion was not only a direct challenge to President Ahmadinejad but to the authority of the Supreme Leader.

With regard to the prevailing view of *velayat-e faghih*, in the democratic scenario this factor would create a foundational justification for the Supreme Leader to assume a more benevolent role as a chief of state with more accountability to the public. The concept of a democratic *velayat-e faghih* would have a stronger influence than the absolutist or quietist readings. Debates over *velayat-e faghih* would become more open during the time of succession, and government responses to

---

11   Kamal Nazer Yasin, "Iran: Rafsanjani Presses Political Offensive Against President, Stressing Moderation," EurasiaNet, February 21, 2007.

alternative interpretations would be muted. One might see such indicators as key Qom ayatollahs becoming more vocal in their criticism of Khamenei's religious legitimacy, without censure by the government. Disputes over various interpretations of *velayat-e faghih* among clerics could also be increasingly aired in public. Such discussions might extend to meetings of the Assembly of Experts, as clerical statements about the need to incorporate popular will in the national interest became more frequent.

In this trajectory, Khamenei's personal network would experience a diminution of its influence and power, which would, in turn, lessen its ability to manipulate succession. Groups and individuals in the personal network would bow to political and societal pressures to retreat from previous activities. Among the indicators would be the appearance of schisms within the Revolutionary Guards related to personal enrichment and involvement in Iranian politics. Such a development would pressure Khamenei to enforce the view that the military should avoid interfering in the political system, leading to a reining in of the Guards' involvement in politics. In addition, one might see Khamenei replace certain key Guards leaders, widely considered ideologues, who were advocating that the Guards' domestic powers be expanded. More broadly, government initiatives would appear to improve accountability within Khamenei's personal network. For example, special government and Majles committees could be set up to account for *bonyad* activities and income.

In sum, the balance of factional power and *velayat-e faghih* would supersede Khamenei's personal network as factors shaping a succession that led to a democratic Supreme Leader. Relaxation of government-imposed restrictions on opposition factions and the rise of the democratic interpretation of *velayat-e faghih*—along with new alliances between pragmatic conservatives, reformists, and some principlist elements—would combine with a weakening of Khamenei's personal network to make the next succession a more democratic, constitutionally based process. Decisionmaking would be more inclusive, and the Assembly of Experts would likely have a dominant role. One might see, for instance, the assembly and Majles forming a group to revise the constitution to strengthen republican institutions and make the

Supreme Leader position more accountable. A temporary leadership council might be formed on the basis of guidance from the Expediency Council. At that point, with the Guards somewhat weakened politically, Islamist Left and pragmatic Islamist Right factions might join with pro-democratic *velayat-e faghih* clerics to propose a reformist cleric as a candidate. The Assembly of Experts could then vote for that candidate in a public ceremony.

In this scenario, the Islamic Revolution would remain the point of reference for the Supreme Leader and the *nezam*, but the Islamist Left's preferred reading of *velayat-e faghih* would dominate. Accordingly, the Supreme Leader would not be able to justify his position solely on the basis of divine authority; his authority would also derive from popular will. There would be more open political participation in selecting the next Supreme Leader and greater oversight after he took office, with the Assembly of Experts and Majles more active in overseeing his performance than is the case today. The central role played by the Supreme Leader's popularity in maintaining his position would more closely resemble the concept of the *marja*, who attains his religious stature by virtue of numbers of adherents. Notably, in the democratic scenario, the Revolutionary Guards would no longer provide a foundation for the Supreme Leader's political power and influence. Instead, the Guards' leadership would be purged of revolutionary hardliners, who would be replaced by commanders forbidden from engaging in internal politics. The *nezam* would link this ban on politicization of the Revolutionary Guards to Khomeini's admonition that the military "obey the laws regarding the prevention of the military forces from entering into politics."[12]

In general, less power and influence would be concentrated in the hands of the Supreme Leader in the democratic scenario than in the status quo case, with a commensurate amount of decisionmaking responsibility passing to the republican institutions of the state. The Supreme Leader would remain the highest authority in the land, but checks and balances would be in place to ensure that elected officials would be formally consulted on critical matters of state. His world-

---

[12] Wehrey et al., 2009a, p. 78.

view would be less important in the formulation of security policy: He would remain the commander in chief, and there would be a single line of command and control under him, but he would share some national security authority with the president and his ministers (including formal consultation over the hiring and firing of military commanders and development of national security strategy). A lowered profile for his special representatives would limit his ability to control the *nezam* through informal levers of influence. He would no longer control the electoral process through the Guardian Council, which might be curtailed or even eliminated. Key elements of the Supreme Leader's personal network—including the Office of the Supreme Leader, the Revolutionary Guards, and the *bonyads*—would be held accountable before the law and elected institutions.

While the Islamic Revolution would remain the foundation of the *nezam*, it would no longer occupy a large part of political discourse in Iran. Revolutionary rhetoric would wane in favor of pragmatism and "normal-state" concerns. Iran's independence and status on the regional and global stages would still be very important, but its Islamic revolutionary pedigree would become less of an underlying factor in political discourse on foreign policy than Iranian nationalism. In the democratic scenario, the Supreme Leader's personal ideological beliefs, while still important, would be less dominant in the domestic and foreign policies of the state than in the status quo or absolutist scenarios. However, these ideological beliefs would lean toward a more open view of societal norms and the outside world, including the West.

This scenario would require the constitution of 1989 to be substantially revised. As much emphasis would be given to the people's acceptance of the next Supreme Leader as to requirements related to scholarship, piety, and other qualifications. The Supreme Leader's duties and powers would be further elaborated to clearly differentiate his responsibilities from those of the president. There would be stipulations that the Supreme Leader should consult with the president and the Majles in delineating and executing general policies of the state. The supervisory role of the Assembly of Experts would likely be strengthened and its deliberations made public.

The Supreme Leader in the democratic scenario would be a relatively high-ranking cleric (possibly even a *marja*) with reformist or pragmatic conservative leanings who may not have been a *nezam* "insider." Indeed, he could be drawn from outside the "men's club" that has ruled the Islamic Republic since the revolution. He would be a popular religious leader among large segments of the population. He would be a social conservative himself but would be willing to accommodate elements of modernism in Iranian society. A cleric like Grand Ayatollah Sanei might be a suitable candidate.

Regarding the country's internal politics, the political system of the Islamic Republic would be more inclusive in this scenario than it is today, with a more vibrant civil society and a weakening of patronage networks. At the same time, factionalism could be more acute, and the Supreme Leader would no longer take the role of "arbiter." Some factions, especially on the right, could find themselves outside the system and could become a potentially destabilizing force. Because of this, some violence could occur, carried out by underground, right-wing vigilante groups and quietly endorsed by radical clerics and former Revolutionary Guards elements. The Supreme Leader would remain dependent on informal networks, but reformists, pragmatic conservatives, and other moderate groups like the Association of Combative Clergymen would dominate them. The *nezam* would focus less on "Islamic values" (e.g., dress codes) and countering Western cultural influence and more on economic progress and rule of law.

Leadership Council: An Executive Body Beholden to Qom

The Leadership Council scenario would mirror the democratic scenario, in the sense that it would shift the balance of influence over state matters away from the Supreme Leader and toward Iran's elected institutions and the popular will. But, in contrast, Qom and the broader clerical class would play a more important role in decisionmaking. The idea of replacing a single Supreme Leader with this sort of executive body has been discussed at various times over the course of the Islamic Republic's three-decade history. Both Rafsanjani and the late Grand Ayatollah Montazeri, for example, have raised the idea of a leadership council composed of senior clerics, which would dilute the concept of an absolute *velayat-e faghih* and allow them and their followers a greater say in decisionmaking—especially after Khamenei passes from the scene. In his December 2008 speech, Rafsanjani proposed a Fatwa Council made up of Iran's *marjas*.[13] Though not strictly a leadership council, Rafsanjani's proposal resembled a system of government based on collective decisionmaking by the clergy. The notion of a permanent council also appeared in the 1979 constitution.[14] Generally, proponents of the concept have hailed from the reformist and pragmatic conservative camps of the *nezam*; principlists would most likely oppose the idea.[15]

In the Leadership Council scenario, the balance of factional power would follow a course over the next two to three years similar to that of the democratic scenario. However, factional competition—among reformist groups and between cross-factional alliances—could be more acute. For example, reformists might form clear subfactions because of disagreements over strategy and state policy. Cross-factional alliances might form over more distinct issues. Some of this factional debate could take place in the Assembly of Experts, which, as in the trajectory toward the democratic scenario, could emerge as a more-active institution in debating the role of the Supreme Leader and influencing succession. At the same time, clerics in Qom would take a more-dominant position in policy debates. The clergy would generally broaden discussion about the nature of the institution of Supreme Leader and whether a single person can hold the position, given the lack of an iconic figure like Khomeini. Moreover, calls might be made for the institution of Supreme Leader to be more representative of the entire clerical class.

With regard to the prevailing view of *velayat-e faghih*, the Islamist Left (and pragmatic conservative) interpretation of the concept would provide the foundation for a Leadership Council to replace a single Supreme Leader. The support of the mainstream clerical establishment

---

[13] Yasin, 2009.

[14] See Algar, 1980a, pp. 66–69.

[15] Rafsanjani's views on Shi'a jurisprudence (*ijtehad*) and *velayat-e faghih* are widely reflected within the ideology of groups like the *Kargozaran-e Sazandegi*, which favor a more-circumscribed role for the Supreme Leader (Moslem, 2002, p. 131).

in Qom would likely strengthen the religious legitimacy of the Islamic Republic. Qom would influence the Leadership Council through informal networks, as well as the Assembly of Experts.

In terms of Khamenei's personal network, this factor, too, would develop in a manner similar to that in the democratic scenario: The network's influence and power would diminish, lessening its ability to determine succession. Here, factionalism and *velayat-e faghih* would also be the dominant factors. But factional competition, an inability to find a single compromise candidate, and broader support for a "shared" leadership would propel succession toward a Leadership Council. Various factions and associated clerical groups might each propose strong candidates for Supreme Leader—all respected ayatollahs with democratic-leaning views of *velayat-e faghih.*

The council would consist of three to five clerics who were to some extent accountable both to Qom and to elected institutions. The Assembly of Experts would elect and supervise members of the council. The council as a whole would have the same responsibilities and authorities as a single democratic Supreme Leader and would share decision-making with elected institutions to a greater extent than in the status quo scenario. The council would rule by consensus, but each member could possibly retain a specific portfolio (e.g., economic development, social development, etc.) for matters of state in which he would have additional responsibilities and authorities. One cleric might become a "first among equals," who would hold the most important portfolio—national security—and serve as the commander in chief but who would have to consult with the other members of the council on all matters. The council would also consult with the president and Majles.

As in the democratic scenario, revolutionary ideology would be less prevalent in state policymaking than in the status quo scenario. Viewpoints on the outside world, particularly the United States and the West, would be wide-ranging, with the views of the member who had been designated "first among equals" tending to drive the consensus of the council on this topic.

Changes to the 1989 constitution would be similar to those described in the democratic scenario. However, the constitution would now define the Leadership Council as a permanent body, rather than as a transitional body, and references to a single Supreme Leader would be removed. It would provide details of the composition of the council and define the state portfolios each member is to retain, as well as the relationships between the council members and the president, his ministers, and the Majles. The Guardian Council might be eliminated, and the Assembly of Experts would be constitutionally empowered to elect, actively supervise, and dismiss members of the council.

The Leadership Council members would be high-ranking clerics drawn from both inside and outside the "men's club." These clerics would tend to be socially conservative, but their factional tendencies would run the gamut from reformist to pragmatic conservative to traditional conservative. Principlist-leaning clerics, however, would not participate and would be considered as outside the "system" because of their adherence to the concept of a single leader and view of an absolute *velayat-e faghih*. Each council member would likely demonstrate acumen in matters of state policy and administration. Ayatollah Rafsanjani would be a possible candidate for membership.

With regard to internal political dynamics, policymaking would likely be more dysfunctional than in other scenarios because of the existence of multiple personalities on the council and the continued prevalence of factionalism.

Abolition: Demise of the Islamic Republic

A final possible scenario would revolve around the abolition of the office of Supreme Leader. Taking its place would be either a secular republic or an Islamist republic not led by clergy.[16] Here the nature of leadership would shift from theocracy with trappings of democracy to some other form of government. This scenario could reflect the interests of secular forces in Iranian society. But it could also be driven by nonclerical Islamist forces, especially the Revolutionary Guards. It

---

[16] It is not our intent to detail multiple alternatives to the current political system, although we provide examples where helpful. Additionally, it is important to note that one might not see the configuration of factors that would lead up to the abolition scenario until Khamenei passes from the scene (either naturally or by force), and they could evolve relatively quickly.

would make plain that *velayat-e faghih* and republicanism are diametrically opposed systems of government.

In this scenario, the three key factors that would shape the next succession in the other four scenarios would evolve dramatically enough to negate the concept of a Supreme Leader. First, factional competition as it is currently known would cease to play a decisive role in determining the Iranian political landscape. Instead, alternative political tendencies—secularists, nationalists, leftists, and various groups within Iranian civil society—would either be expressed as recognized political parties or associations in an expanded civil society or suppressed in a one-party or no-party system. Competition among groups would take place on a different playing field (perhaps a democracy) and with rules that were markedly different from those of the *nezam*. Political groups would likely form along lines similar to those groups that helped Khomeini overthrow the Shah but that were ultimately repressed and silenced after the revolution because of the obstacles they presented to the implementation of Khomeini's *velayat-e faghih*. There were four such broad groups:

- The **secular nationalists**, especially those organized under the banner of the pro-Mossadegh National Front, had the distinction of being one of the oldest and, at times, most prestigious opposition groups against the Shah.
- The **Islamist nationalists** attempted to fill the vacuum between Iranian nationalism and Islamism. Members of the Islamist nationalist Freedom Movement of Iran formed Khomeini's core group of advisors during his exile in France just before the Islamic Revolution and took an active role in setting the revolution in motion. But they constituted a key segment of the revolutionary opposition to Khomeini's *velayat-e faghih*.
- The **Islamist and secular leftists/Marxists** included such groups as the Mujaheddin-e Khalq organization.
- The **traditionalist Shi'a clergy** challenged Khomeini's concept of *velayat-e faghih*, calling it an illegitimate concept of Shi'a governance.

With regard to *velayat-e faghih*, it would lose all status as the political foundation of the state. Absolutist and democratic views of *velayat-e faghih* would be largely abandoned in Qom and elsewhere in Iran in favor of the quietist view. Reasons provided for its demise might include Khamenei's use of it to justify authoritarian rule and even the perception that Khomeini had reinterpreted what had been a religious concept to attain political power.[17]

As for Khamenei's personal network, certain elements would become less powerful and would be unable to prevent—or might even be willing to support—the abolition of the Supreme Leader position and the Islamic Republic. An important indicator would be powerful and influential figures willingly reducing or eliminating ties to Khamenei. For example, the leadership of the Revolutionary Guards might openly defy the Supreme Leader, first on minor issues and eventually on more substantive policy ones. A powerful lay leader with a personal network that was somewhat independent of Khamenei's network might offer a vision of the future that contradicted the *nezam*'s principles. Alliances among groups and networks outside the *nezam* could broaden and strengthen, leading to common goals between the bazaar and the Green Movement, for example. At the same time, other elements of the Supreme Leader's personal network might weaken as, for example, his representatives were pushed out or isolated from key institutions and Friday prayer leaders gave sermons that did not follow government dictates.

In short, in the abolition scenario, all three factors would become less relevant in relation to other forces. The abolition of the Supreme Leader position would coincide with a reversion of *velayat-e faghih* to the traditional quietist interpretation of the role of the clergy in government. The republic would likely be based on secular or Islamist-nationalist principles. The clerical establishment would play only a minor role in statecraft and might publicly assert its position only when it saw a dire threat to Islam and the *umma*, which could be relatively infre-

---

[17] As a *marja*, Khomeini was able to claim *velayat-e faghih* as Shi'a religious doctrine, but Khamenei's lower religious status and overpoliticization of the concept has weakened the religious value of the concept and made it vulnerable to future challenges.

quently. With a Supreme Leader no longer the chief of state, the head of state—quite possibly the president—would assume the responsibilities of commander in chief. Bifurcation in the system would no longer exist, and executive power would reside in the republican institutions.

Nationalism could very possibly replace religious tendencies as the predominant ideological component of Iranian policymaking and political discourse, especially under a secular republic. While the new government's view of the outside world is impossible to predict, it would almost certainly retain a strong sense that Iran should play an important, if not dominant, role in regional affairs.

The constitution in the abolition scenario would be completely revised. A different political-ideological concept that did not include the office of the Supreme Leader would be written into the document. Constitutional articles would describe rights, responsibilities, and authorities accordingly. Sharia law could be enshrined as shaping all laws, particularly in the Islamist-nationalist case. But its centrality (i.e., whether it was the highest authority or merely supplemented secular law) would depend on the form of government.

Regardless of what form of government would replace the Supreme Leader, candidates for chief of state would very likely be laypeople, not clerics. In some cases, they might be from military circles. It is least likely that a candidate would be a member of the "men's club" and more likely that he would be a member of the Revolutionary Guards or a member of the new Green Movement.

Power would be centralized in a single leader and bureaucracy. Still, informal networks, which thrived under the Shah as well as under the Supreme Leader, would remain a prevalent part of the Iranian political landscape. Other developments in Iran's political dynamics would depend on the type of government. For example, under a representative secular government, civil society could strengthen and a less-ideological system could emerge. The government would pursue more-"rational," coherent policymaking. Alternatively, an authoritarian or military government would severely weaken civil society and curtail basic freedoms. In this case, factions or parties might exist, but they would be restrained by the government. It might be declared, for example, that only one party was permitted to rule.

The "Wild Card" Factor: The Nature and Timing of Khamenei's Exit

In addition to the three key factors, how and when Khamenei departs the scene will also influence the type of leadership that follows him. In the event that he dies suddenly—especially if he has not chosen a successor—the Islamic Republic may have a difficult time ensuring a smooth succession process. Unlike Khomeini, who had named Montazeri as his successor and quickly chose Khamenei as a replacement once Montazeri was disqualified, Khamenei has not indicated a preference for his successor. It is possible that he has decided on the choice of successor privately, hoping to reveal the decision shortly before his passing; this would prevent any undermining of his authority while he is still in power. But if his preference is unknown, his sudden passing may create an intense struggle over succession.

In contrast, should Khamenei pass away due to a long illness or deterioration in health, the succession process may be smoother. In this case, Khamenei might make a decision as to who should succeed him while obtaining the cooperation of various power centers and political actors in the Islamic Republic. But should he announce a personal choice for his successor (which would almost certainly favor the principlists), public knowledge of his passing, or even that limited to the elite, would then possibly increase the friction between competing factions and power centers. The reformists and the pragmatic conservatives would be likely to make strong efforts to shape succession if they knew Khamenei was passing away, most likely concentrating their efforts on rallying enough support in the Assembly of Experts to select a Supreme Leader who would protect their interests. At the same time, hard-line principlists such as Mesbah-Yazdi could attempt to dominate the assembly in order to shape the succession in their favor. Elements of the Revolutionary Guards, who would want to prevent the reformists and pragmatic conservatives, such as Rafsanjani, from assuming the highest position of power, might aid Mesbah-Yazdi and his principlist counterparts. If faced with this, the reformists and pragmatic conservatives would probably find it more difficult to shape succession, even if they were to have a substantial presence in the assembly and the support of a significant section of the clergy in Qom.

The Status Quo and Absolutist Scenarios Seem the Most Likely for the Next Succession

The post-election alignment of the three factors in 2011—with the hard-right principlist faction continuing to dominate elected institutions, *velayat-e faghih* appearing to be a less decisive influence, and Khamenei's personal network acting forcefully to protect the status quo—suggests strongly that the most likely succession scenario within the next two to three years is the status quo. The absolutist scenario is a close second. The other three scenarios are much less likely in the near term.

Yet those three scenarios are not entirely out of the realm of possibility. With regard to the democratic and Leadership Council scenarios, Iran's various factions—including the reformists and the pragmatic conservatives—will likely challenge the ruling principlist faction during the time of succession. Although these "opposition" factions are locked out of power for now, there is a chance that they could gain the support of institutions not closely aligned with Khamenei, Ahmadinejad, and the top echelon of the Revolutionary Guards. Indeed, one such institution, the Assembly of Experts, would likely be the key to any possibility of one of these two near-term scenarios coming to pass. Historically, the assembly has played a rather marginal role in Iranian politics and the Islamic Republic's previous succession decision. If that stays the same, it would seemingly serve as a rubber-stamp body for Khamenei's choice of successor. But given its current leader, Rafsanjani, it is not impossible that it could have a much more telling influence. The assembly chose Rafsanjani as its chief in 2007. Some regard this as a rebuke to the principlists, their view of an absolute *velayat-e faghih*, and Khamenei's role as Supreme Leader. Khamenei's personal pick for the position is reported to have been the ultra-conservative head of the Guardian Council, Ayatollah Ali Jannati.[18] Yet, in contrast with Jannati's 36 votes, 41 members of the assembly voted for Rafsanjani. Rafsanjani's subsequent reelection to the post in 2009 was seen as "a heavy defeat for the anti-Rafsanjani trend,"[19] reconfirming the assembly's support for him and his political views—even possibly for his position on *velayat-e faghih* and the Supreme Leader. In this sense, the assembly could exercise its constitutional role in selecting the next Supreme Leader more assertively, making a proactive choice based on an alternative view of *velayat-e faghih*. Either selecting a democratic Supreme Leader or replacing the Supreme Leader with a Leadership Council would be options. The near-term political fortunes of Rafsanjani and his political allies among the moderate Islamist Right and the traditional clergy will determine the assembly's role in a succession in the next several years.

Yet there are countervailing forces that make these scenarios far less likely to come about than the status quo or absolutist cases. The Leadership Council scenario may not be very viable in the near future because it might involve a higher level of dysfunctionality in policymaking than in other scenarios. Iran currently faces serious domestic and international challenges, ranging from contention over the presidential elections to increased U.S. and international sanctions in response to Iran's ongoing nuclear program. Unified, efficient decisionmaking will be essential to address these challenges. Further, the hardline Islamist Right—particularly principlists within Khamenei's inner circle and the Revolutionary Guards—will surely strongly object to a Leadership Council that might include figures from the Islamist Left and *marjas* who are opposed to the absolute *velayat-e faghih*. As for the possibility that an alternative view of *velayat-e faghih* could take prominence, despite being theoretically and religiously sound, the democratic interpretation has dim prospects for implementation during the

---

[18]   Author discussion with former Iranian government official, January 2008. According to this official, Sadegh Larijani (former member of the Guardian Council, Ali Larijani's brother, and newly appointed chief of the judiciary) had informed assembly members that Jannati was Khamenei's choice, but they ultimately ignored this recommendation.

[19]   "Shekast-e Sangin-e Jaryan-e Zed Hashemi; Ou Rais Mand" [A Heavy Defeat for the Anti-Rafsanjani Trend; He Remains as Chief], Entekhab News, March 10, 2009.

next succession: The Islamist Left, which advocates this interpretation, no longer has the clout and authority to exert a decisive influence on the succession process, especially in the near term. It appears that this will remain the case for the foreseeable future.

The abolition scenario also seems unlikely in the near term. Today, the quietist clergy maintain a strong presence in Qom and throughout Iran's religious hierarchy. But they do not play an active role in decisionmaking and politics in the Islamic Republic. In addition, there are no signs at the moment that key elements of Khamenei's personal network intend to oppose his will or are interested in an alternative system. The leadership of the Revolutionary Guards remains deeply committed to the Supreme Leader and the *nezam*, particularly since the Guards' power and influence on decisionmaking appear to have expanded since the 2009 election. The Revolutionary Guards may see its influence grow further in the context of a status quo succession. The principlists, too, seem to be consolidating their own political power and would likely see abolition as a threat to their recent gains. Finally, the Green Movement appears neither inclined nor poised in the near term to foment a major uprising that would threaten Khamenei's rule or might overturn the *nezam*, should he pass away.

CHAPTER SIX

Succession of the Supreme Leader in the Longer Term

Although the most likely shorter-term outlook for the next Supreme Leader seems relatively clear, succession may very well not take place within the next few years. Ali Khamenei is 71 years old.[1] Shi'a ayatollahs tend to have a long average life span that extends into their 80s or 90s; Khamenei is relatively young by comparison. While he is rumored to have health problems, the current Supreme Leader could live a long life yet and could remain in his position for quite some time. Uncertainty about the succession increases exponentially the further into the future one looks. For one thing, the effects of the 2009 election will be much different over the next decade or two than within the next few years. In addition, other forces will be at play that will significantly alter the context—political, economic, and societal—in which the *nezam* makes decisions, as well as the configuration of the three key factors. If succession occurs in ten, 15, or even 20 years, it is much more difficult to forecast its nature.

The Longer-Term Effects of the 2009 Election

In the longer term, Khamenei's actions during the dispute over the 2009 presidential election may have weakened both his personal religious and political legitimacy and the authority of the office he has

---

[1]   As of January 2011.

occupied for two decades. The election revealed deep divisions between the *nezam*'s current leadership, the clerical establishment, and the Iranian people. Over time, countervailing forces may persist that could threaten the vision Khamenei and his network have for the Islamic Republic.

A number of senior clerics, including *marjas* with greater religious legitimacy than Khamenei himself, have expressed considerable dissatisfaction with the way Khamenei handled the election, his support for Ahmadinejad, the validity of the results, and Ahmadinejad himself. Several prominent figures in this group, including Sanei and Montazeri, strongly criticized the government's response. Ayatollah Jalaleddin Taheri, former Friday prayer leader of Isfahan and a consistent critic of the *nezam*, went so far as to declare the election result "void and false."[2] Rafsanjani's reaction can also be seen as reflecting the frustration of this segment of the top-ranking clergy with the Supreme Leader. In his Friday prayer speech at Tehran University on June 17, 2009, Rafsanjani blamed the Guardian Council, the body which formalized Ahmadinejad's reelection by discounting claims of widespread electoral fraud, for wasting the time "given to them to talk to the ulema" about the post-election "crisis."[3] "Why," he asked rhetorically, "should our Sources of Emulation who always have been supportive, and our seminary schools, which have never had any expectations for their efforts, be upset today?"[4] In criticizing the Guardian Council so blatantly, Rafsanjani indirectly pointed an incriminating finger at Khamenei.

The antipathy of these senior clerics for Ahmadinejad in particular has a history. Ahmadinejad has challenged the religious authority of the Iranian clerical establishment with accusations of corruption and claims that he was in direct communication with the *Mahdi*. He appears to view himself as paving the way for the return of the Hidden Imam. His claims of being in communication with the *Mahdi* under-

---

2   Asre Nou, "In Entekhabat Ra Makhdoosh va An Ra Batel va Tasdi Mojadad Rais Dolat Ra Baray Dor e Baed Na Mashroo va Ghasbaneh Midanam [I Consider This Election to Be Null and Void]," Asre Nou News, July 2009.

3   "Iran: Full Text of Rafsanjani's Lengthy Speech," 2009.

4   "Iran: Full Text of Rafsanjani's Lengthy Speech," 2009.

mine the legitimacy and even the necessity of Iran's clerical class, who have long been seen to serve as "guardians" of the masses until the Hidden Imam reemerges from his occultation. Ahmadinejad has buttressed his own religious-political power not only by implicitly questioning the clergy's religious authority but also by explicitly attacking their political role within the Islamic Republic.[5] In so doing, he has actually weakened the concept of *velayat-e faghih* as Iran's dominant ideology. While there are still senior clergymen, such as Ayatollahs Mesbah-Yazdi and Jannati, who support Ahmadinejad and his policies, they are in the minority; he does not have the backing of most.

Khamenei's consistent support for Ahmadinejad since 2005 has been seen by some camps as having colluded in, or at least acquiesced to, this weakening of *velayat-e faghih* at the expense of Iran's traditional clerical class. Over this period, Khamenei has not based his rule on the advice or consensus of the broader clergy. Instead, he has in some ways acted in a more *secular* manner, leading a growing number of clerics to view his decisions as no longer serving *velayat-e faghih* or the *nezam* but as furthering the interests of a narrow group of the ruling elite, including his personal network and elements of the Revolutionary Guards. When he so vocally supported Ahmadinejad in 2009, deep rifts between the Supreme Leader and the clerical class based in Qom could no longer be covered over. Many senior clergymen—and not only those who support the quietist or democratic vision of *velayat-e faghih*—today appear to have lost trust in Khamenei as the Islamic Republic's highest political *and* religious authority.

Over the longer term, Khamenei's actions may very well have important consequences. He may be Iran's official supreme religious authority, but, nevertheless, he still requires the acknowledgment and approval of the country's clerical establishment—especially given his often-questioned religious qualifications. His gradual loss of support among certain senior Qom clergy will, over time, likely further erode his religious credentials as Iran's Supreme Leader and, consequently, undermine his long-term influence.

---

5   Ahmadinejad has been linked with the anticlerical Hojjatieh Society.

These traditional members of the clergy in Qom may join the reformist and the pragmatic conservative factions that form the opposition to Ahmadinejad's presidency as the principal source of resistance to whomever Khamenei's personal network chooses to be the next Supreme Leader. But that choice may even face strong opposition from some of the very traditional conservatives and principlists who have traditionally supported Khamenei's leadership and the absolutist *velayat-e faghih*. Much of this opposition may stem from disagreements over policies, personalities, and "styles" of management rather than ideology or discourse on the *velayat-e faghih*. Conservative and principlist leaders, such as Ali Larijani, have not hidden their discontent with Ahmadinejad's performance as president. By supporting Ahmadinejad so vigorously, Khamenei may have alienated some of these core supporters, even among such conservative organizations as the *Motalefeh* and the SCC. Given the nature of Iranian politics, some of these key conservative figures and associations may also shift their ideological position on *velayat-e faghih* if their political and economic interests are not being met.

Such resistance from elements of the Islamist Right, combined with opposition from the Islamist Left and broad segments of the Iranian population dissatisfied with the status quo and Khamenei as ruler, may over time erode his clout and standing to such a degree that he and his personal network will be unable to manage the selection of the next Supreme Leader. Khamenei's network and principlists of the Revolutionary Guards may hold the levers of power today. But even they will not be able to ignore potential resistance from the clergy, Iran's broader revolutionary establishment, and the Iranian people.

The Configuration of the Three Factors Will Change

Regarding succession further into the future, the balance of factions, informal networks, and power centers in the Islamic Republic will likely change in ways that are difficult to predict. This goes to the heart of the configuration of all three key factors but particularly of Khamenei's personal network and the factional balance of power. Our previous research on Iranian leadership dynamics suggests that there has been a cyclical ebb and flow of power and influence since the Islamic Revolution.[6] One group or power center seems to dominate politically and/or economically over a given period, only to be eclipsed at some point by another group that emerges as a locus of influence.

The Revolutionary Guards are currently the dominant political and economic power center, with the 2009 presidential election seeming to have cemented their position. However, while it is difficult to see their power waning in the next two to three years, it is not a foregone conclusion that they will still be dominant in ten years, for example. Although the top echelons of the Guards support Khamenei, Ahmadinejad, and the more hard-line principlist ideology of the Islamist Right, the Guards overall are not a monolithic organization, a point demonstrated by reported purges of more-moderate Guards commanders.[7] But should they continue to focus on business ventures and economic power, as they are currently doing, this could eventually affect their outlook, making them more averse to risk and apt to seek regional stability. It could also set the conditions for an alternative power center to emerge that challenges the Guards' dominance of Iranian politics.

Other Factors Will Also Influence Succession in the Longer Term

In addition to the three key factors, other variables will evolve in ways that are hard to determine. The *nezam* can influence some of these changes; others are largely beyond its control.

The "Old Guard" Will Disappear and Be Replaced

First, the "old guard," whose several dozen members helped bring the Islamic Revolution to fruition and who have held positions of power

---

[6] See Thaler et al., 2010, pp. 55–67, 126–127.

[7] "The Revolutionary Guards: Gaining Power in Iran," *Time*, August 13, 2009. See also Wehrey et al., 2009a, and Thaler et al., 2010, p. 66.

and influence in the Islamic Republic ever since, will be gone. In ten to 20 years, a new cadre of leaders, many of whom came of age during the Iran-Iraq War, will have replaced their elders. They will bring to their positions a different perception of the Islamic Republic and different life experiences. Some in this new generation are associated with the rise of the Revolutionary Guards and already are challenging the "old guard," particularly the clerical members. Ahmadinejad's use of messianic imagery in his rhetoric and denunciation of alleged corruption among and enrichment of key clerics can be viewed in this light.[8] A new generation of Islamist Leftists will also emerge, as will a younger cadre of clerics, whose political tendencies and relationship with the *nezam* will differ from those of the older generation of opposition leaders. The political worldviews of the new generation of leaders will likely cast the role of the Supreme Leader in a different light than the one in which their elders viewed it.

Domestic Issues Will Inevitably Evolve, Putting Pressure on the *Nezam* to Adapt

More generally, economic, societal, cultural, and other endogenous issues will continue to put pressure on the *nezam* to adapt to changing realities. Among the most prominent concerns are providing job opportunities to a youthful population, considering the demands of Iran's women's rights movement, and dealing with the burgeoning information revolution. These and other issues will challenge the *nezam* either to meet the expanding needs of the population at the risk of modernizing its current ideological tendencies or to ignore and suppress popular will at the risk of further polarizing society and increasingly alienating the population from the government. Regardless of the preferences of

---

[8]   In June 2008, Abbas Palizdar, a presumed supporter of Ahmadinejad and member of the Majles Judicial Inquiry and Review Committee, publicly accused such members of the clerical elite as Rafsanjani, Ayatollah Mohammad Yazdi, Ayatollah Nateq Nouri, and Ayatollah Mohammad Enami Kashani (Tehran's provisional Friday prayer leader) of using their influence in the government for personal profit. Ahmadinejad soon distanced himself from the accusations, and Palizdar was jailed. See "The Accuser Is Accused, and Jailed," *Iran Press Service*, June 11, 2008; and Thomas Erdbrink, "Iran Official Arrested for Criticizing Clerics," *Washington Post*, June 12, 2008, p. A14.

Khamenei and the *nezam* for what follows Khamenei's passing, these pressures will likely influence the longer-term context in which succession might occur.

Iran's Relationship with the United States Will Play a Role

Lastly, should Khamenei continue to rule for many years, relations between Iran and the United States could affect the type of Supreme Leader that follows Khamenei. The ultimate outcome of the ongoing confrontation between the United States and Iran over the Islamic Republic's nuclear program will play a critical role in determining this relationship. But other issues like human rights, Iran's support for terrorism, and prospects for peace or continued conflict between Israel and its Palestinian and other Arab neighbors will exert an influence as well. A "history" is yet to be written on this relationship over the next decade or so, and it will undoubtedly inform the succession. Will the United States continue to lead a movement to isolate or "contain" Iran marked by a confrontational relationship? Will there have been a military confrontation between Iran and the United States or Israel over the nuclear program? Or, despite the current pessimism about U.S. relations with Iran, will a process for U.S.-Iranian rapprochement be under way at the time of succession? Any one of these future "histories" would influence who or what follows Khamenei in ten to 15 years.

CHAPTER SEVEN

Concluding Remarks

In this report, we have sought to provide analysts with a solid, well-defined set of factors, indicators, and possible end states for succession to the current Supreme Leader that will help them interpret trends regarding the future of the Islamic Republic. The five scenarios and the trajectories that lead to them are based on a historical evaluation of three key factors that we believe will determine the nature of the next Supreme Leader or even the possibility that the position may be abolished. While it will remain impossible to predict the exact direction Iran will take after Khamenei's passing, the framework and tools we provide here should help the United States better prepare for a new era in Iran if Khamenei leaves the scene in the next two to three years.

The Supreme Leader stands at the center of the Islamic Republic, exerting a decisive influence on its character, policies, and worldview. Khamenei has held the position for more than two-thirds of the Islamic Republic's existence. His departure will mark a fundamental change. Even a succession that results in something like the status quo scenario may be characterized by fluctuations in leadership dynamics, as various power centers and factions challenge the new Supreme Leader.

Many Iranians believe political change in their country is long overdue. The Islamic Revolution succeeded in overthrowing a repressive and anachronistic system of government. Yet it has failed to address in a satisfactory way the needs and desires of Iran's dynamic and vibrant society, which has undergone a vast transformation since 1979. The current Supreme Leader, Ayatollah Khamenei, and his relatively small group of supporters within the political system now stand in the way of such change. His passing will prove to be a critical moment in Iran's future and its relationship with the United States.

Bibliography

Abdo, Geneive, "Re-Thinking the Islamic Republic: A Conversation with Ayatollah Hossein Ali Montazeri," *Middle East Journal*, Winter 2001.

"The Accuser Is Accused, and Jailed," Iran Press Service, June 11, 2008.

Amidi, Faranak, "Rezaei: Iran Needs Electoral System Change," Indymedia-Lëtzebuerg, November 3, 2008. As of January 20, 2011: http://www.indymedia-letzebuerg.net/index.php?option=com_content&task=view&id=11837&Itemid=28

Ahmadinejad, Mahmoud, "Iran Commentary Speaks on Different Approaches to Revolution," BBC Monitoring, March 11, 2008.

Akhavi, Shahrough, "The Thought and Role of Ayatollah Hossein'ali Montazeri in the Politics of Post-1979 Iran," *Iranian Studies*, December 1, 2008.

Alfoneh, Ali, "What Do Structural Changes in the Guards Mean?" American Enterprise Institute, September 2008.

Algar, Hamid, trans., *Constitution of the Islamic Republic of Iran*, Berkeley, Calif.: Mizan Press, 1980a.

———, *Islam and Revolution: Writings and Declarations of Imam Khomeini*, Berkeley, Calif.: Mizan Press, 1980b.

Bakhash, Shaul, *The Reign of the Ayatollahs, Iran and the Islamic Factional Politics in Post-Khomeini Iran*, New York: Basic Books, 1986.

Borger, Julian, "Mojtaba Khamenei: Gatekeeper to Iran's Supreme Leader," *The Guardian* (London), June 22, 2009, p. 14.

Bozorgmehr, Kayvan, "Iran: The Great Purge of Friday Prayer Leaders," Rooz Online, July 28, 2010.

Buchta, Wilfried, *Who Rules Iran? The Structure of Power in the Islamic Republic*, Washington, D.C.: The Washington Institute for Near East Policy and the Konrad-Adenauer-Stiftung, 2000.

Byman, Daniel, Shahram Chubin, Anoushiravan Ehteshami, and Jerrold D. Green, *Iran's Security Policy in the Post-Revolutionary Era*, Santa Monica, Calif.: RAND Corporation, MR-1320-OSD, 2001. As of November 17, 2010: http://www.rand.org/pubs/monograph_reports/MR1320/index.html

Cohen, Roger, "Iran: The Tragedy and the Future," *The New York Review of Books*, August 13, 2009.

Crane, Keith, Rollie Lal, and Jeffrey Martini, *Iran's Political, Demographic, and Economic Vulnerabilities*, Santa Monica, Calif.: RAND Corporation, MG-693-AF, 2008. As of November 17, 2010: http://www.rand.org/pubs/monographs/MG693/

Daraghi, Borzou, "Iran's Revolutionary Guard Acknowledges Taking a Bigger Role in Nation's Security," Lebanon Wire, July 6, 2009. As of July 7, 2009: http://www.lebanonwire.com/0907MLN/09070715LAT.asp

Dareini, Ali Akbar, "Hard-Liners Accuse Top Iranian Cleric of Defiance," Associated Press, July 19, 2009a.

———, "Reformers Call for Probe of Iran Supreme Leader," Associated Press, August 14, 2009b.

Ehteshami, Anoushiravan, *After Khomeini: The Iranian Second Republic*, New York: Routledge, 1995.

Erdbrink, Thomas, "Iran Official Arrested for Criticizing Clerics," *Washington Post*, June 12, 2008, p. A14.

———, "Rallies Close Out Iranian Campaign," *Washington Post*, June 11, 2009.

"Esami Taedadi Az Afsaran e Sepah Ke Az Farman e Khamenei Tamarod Kardand [The Names of a Few Corps Officers Who Disobeyed Khamenei's Command]," CyrusNews.com, July 7, 2009.

Follath, Erich, and Gabor Steingart, "This Iranian Form of Theocracy Has Failed," Spiegel Online International, July 7, 2009. As of August 2009: http://www.spiegel.de/international/world/0,1518,633517,00.html

Green, Jerrold D., Frederic Wehrey, and Charles Wolf, Jr., *Understanding Iran*, Santa Monica, Calif.: RAND Corporation, MG-771-SRF, 2009. As of November 18, 2010: http://www.rand.org/pubs/monographs/MG771/

"Hashemi Rafsanjani: Rouykard Ayatollah Sistani Ba Didgahay-e Ma Hamsan Bood [Ayatollah Sistani's Viewpoint Is the Same as Our Viewpoint]," Mehr News Agency, March 15, 2009.

Hassan-Yari, Houchang, "Iran: Defending the Islamic Revolution—The Corps of the Matter," Eurasianet.org, August 6, 2005. As of November 24, 2010: http://www.eurasianet.org/departments/insight/articles/pp080705.shtml

"Iran: Full Text of Rafsanjani's Lengthy Speech," *Los Angeles Times* web log, June 17, 2009. As of November 24, 2010:
http://latimesblogs.latimes.com/babylonbeyond/2009/07/iranian-cleric-ayatollah-ali-akbar-hashemi-rafsanjani-delivered-what-turned-out-to-be-a-momentous-friday-prayer-sermon-that.html

"Iran University Reform Sparks Row in Ahmadinejad Camp," BBC News, June 23, 2010. As of November 17, 2010:
http://www.bbc.co.uk/news/10390315

"Iranian Dissident Cleric Condemns Government Intimidations," Radio Zamaneh, May 9, 2010. As of January 4, 2011:
http://www.payvand.com/news/10/may/1096.html

"Iran's Rezai Withdraws Election Complaints," Press TV, June 24, 2009.

"Janeshin Namayand e Vali e Faghih dar Sepah, ya Sokhanguy e Hezb e Siyasi Nezamian? [The Deputy Representative of the Supreme Leader in the Guards, or the Spokesperson for the Military Political Party?" Agah Sazi, May 20, 2009. As of January 20, 2011:
http://www.agahsazi.com/article.asp?id=3396&cat=7

Jaquith, Cindy, "Elections Highlight Divisions in Iran's Government," *The Militant*, June 29, 2009.

Kadivar, Mohsen, "This Iranian Form of Theocracy Has Failed," Spiegel Online, July 7, 2001.

Kamdar, Nazanin, "Khamenei's Fatwa About Himself: You Must Obey Me," Rooz Online, July 23, 2010. As of January 4, 2011:
http://www.payvand.com/news/10/jul/1204.html

Kamrava, Mehran, *Iran's Intellectual Revolution*, Cambridge, England: Cambridge University Press, October 27, 2008.

"Karrubi Talks of Constitutional Reform," Rooz Online, April 20, 2009. As of August 24, 2009:
http://www.roozonline.com/english/news3/newsitem/archive/2009/april/20/article/karubi-talks-of-constitutional-reform.html

Khalaji, Mehdi, *The Last Marja: Sistani and the End of Traditional Religious Authority in Shiism*, Washington, D.C.: The Washington Institute for Near East Policy, September 2006.

———, *Apocalyptic Politics: On the Rationality of Iranian Policy*, Washington, D.C.: The Washington Institute for Near East Policy, January 2008.

"Khat Ghermez man Nezam, Imam, va Rahbari Ast ["My Red Line Is the Nezam, Imam, and the Supreme Leadership]," Fars News Agency, April 10, 2009.

Lyon, Alistair, "Analysis—Iran's President Angers Conservatives, Reformists," Reuters, July 19, 2010.

Mesbah-Yazdi, "Rouhaniyat Naboud, Mardom Kafer Mishodand [Without the Clergy, the People Would Become Infidels]," Entekhab News, March 4, 2009.

Moin, Baqer, *Khomeini: Life of the Ayatollah*, New York: Thomas Dunne Books, 1999.

Moslem, Mehdi, *Factional Politics in Post-Khomeini Iran*, Syracuse, N.Y.: Syracuse University Press, 2002.

Naji, Kasra, *Ahmadinejad: The Secret History of Iran's Radical Leader*, Berkeley, Calif.: University of California Press, 2008.

"Nateq-Nouri Thanks Leader for Defending His Reputation," *Tehran Times*, June 22, 2009.

Nou, Asre, "In Entekhabat Ra Makhdoosh va An Ra Batel va Tasdi Mojadad Rais Dolat Ra Baray Dor e Baed Na Mashroo va Ghasbaneh Midanam [I Consider This Election to Be Null and Void]," Asre Nou News, July 2, 2009. As of August 29, 2009:
http://asre-nou.net/php/view.php?objnr=4446

"Principlist Clergy Fail to Endorse Ahmadinejad as Presidential Candidate," Press TV, April 23, 2009. As of August 28, 2009:
http://www.payvand.com/news/09/apr/1256.html

Quran-O-Itrat Academy, "Introduction to Grand Ayatollah Ali Khamenei," undated. As of November 24, 2010:
http://www.qoitrat.org/maraje/default.asp

Rahimi, Babak, *Ayatollah Sistani and the Democratization of Post-Ba'athist Iraq*, Washington, D.C.: United States Institute of Peace, Special Report 187, June 2007.

"The Revolutionary Guards: Gaining Power in Iran," *Time*, August 13, 2009. As of November 24, 2010:
http://www.time.com/time/world/article/0,8599,1915918,00.html

"Rouhani: Jafay e Bozorg Hamiyan Dolat be Rahbar e Enghelab [Rouhani: Government Supporters' Greatest Unkindness Toward the Leader of the Revolution]," Entekhab News, 2008.

Sadjadpour, Karim, *Reading Khamenei: The World View of Iran's Most Powerful Leader*, Washington, D.C.: Carnegie Endowment for International Peace, 2008.

Samii, Bill, "Iran: Early Race For Clerical Assembly Gets Bitter," Radio Free Europe/Radio Liberty, September 22, 2006. As of November 24, 2010:
http://www.rferl.org/content/Article/1071565.html

Sepehri, Vahid, "Iran: Senior Cleric's Death Sparks Search for New Assembly Chairman," Radio Free Europe/Radio Liberty, August 1, 2007. As of November 24, 2010:
http://www.rferl.org/content/article/1077917.html

"Shekast-e Sangin-e Jaryan-e Zed Hashemi; Ou Rais Mand [A Heavy Defeat for the Anti-Rafsanjani Trend; He Remains as Chief]," Entekhab News, March 10, 2009.

Takeyh, Ray, *Hidden Iran: Paradox and Power in the Islamic Republic*, New York: Times Books, 2006.

Thaler, David E., Alireza Nader, Shahram Chubin, Jerrold D. Green, Charlotte Lynch, and Frederic Wehrey, *Mullahs, Guards, and* Bonyads: *An Exploration of Iranian Leadership Dynamics*, Santa Monica, Calif.: RAND Corporation, MG-878-OSD, 2010. As of November 18, 2010:
http://www.rand.org/pubs/monographs/MG878/

"Time to Evaluate Supreme Leadership," Rooz Online, December 30, 2008. As of November 24, 2010:
http://www.roozonline.com/english/news3/newsitem/archive/2008/december/30/article/time-to-evaluate-supreme-leadership.html

Tschentscher, Axel, ed., "Iran: Constitution," International Constitutional Law, 1995. As of 2009:
http://www.servat.unibe.ch/icl/ir00000_.html

"Velayat Faghih Is 'Shirk,' Not Islamic," Rooz Online, December 29, 2008. As of November 24, 2010:
http://www.roozonline.com/english/news3/newsitem/archive/2008/december/29/article/velayat-faghih-is-shirk-not-islamic.html

Wehrey, Frederic, Jerrold D. Green, Brian Nichiporuk, Alireza Nader, Lydia Hansell, Rasool Nafisi, and S. R. Bohandy, *The Rise of the Pasdaran: Assessing the Domestic Roles of the Islamic Revolutionary Guards Corps*, Santa Monica, Calif.: RAND Corporation, MG-821-OSD, 2009a. As of November 18, 2010:
http://www.rand.org/pubs/monographs/MG821/

Wehrey, Frederic, David E. Thaler, Nora Bensahel, Kim Cragin, Jerrold D. Green, Dalia Dassa Kaye, Nadia Oweidat, and Jennifer Li, *Dangerous But Not Omnipotent: Exploring the Reach and Limitations of Iranian Power in the Middle East*, Santa Monica, Calif.: RAND Corporation, MG-781-AF, 2009b. As of November 18, 2010:
http://www.rand.org/pubs/monographs/MG781/

Worth, Robert F., and Nazila Fathi, "Protests Flare in Tehran as Opposition Disputes Vote," *New York Times*, June 13, 2009.

Yasin, Kamal Nazer, "Iran: Rafsanjani Presses Political Offensive Against President, Stressing Moderation," EurasiaNet, February 20, 2007. As of June 1, 2009:
http://www.eurasianet.org/departments/insight/articles/eav022107.shtml

Yasin, Kamal Nazer, "Iran: Rafsanjani at Center of Effort to Promote Reformation of Sh'ia Islam," EurasiaNet, January 29, 2009. As of 2009:
http://www.eurasianet.org/departments/insightb/articles/eav013009.shtml